A YOUNG GIANT PANDA ENJOYS THE VIEW FROM A TREE.

A GIANT PANDA RESTING
BETWEEN BITES OF BAMBOO

NATIONAL GEOGRAPHIC KiDS

Absolute Expert
PANDAS

All the LATEST FACTS From the Field

Ruth Strother

With National Geographic Explorer
Marc Brody

NATIONAL GEOGRAPHIC
Washington, D.C.

CONTENTS

CHAPTER 1
A Bear Like No Other 8

CHAPTER 2
Giant Pandas From Head to Tail 32

MARC BRODY

MARC ENJOYING
TIME OUTDOORS

FOREWORD

Hi! I'm Marc Brody. I'm a conservationist and the president of Panda Mountain and the U.S.-China Environmental Fund. I have spent the last 25 years working to conserve national parks and nature reserves in China. More recently, I have been focused on protecting giant pandas and their habitat.

For as long as I can remember, I have loved wildlife. I take after my grandmother, who talked to me about endangered species and habitat loss. She was fascinated and excited by all kinds of animals, and she loved trees. Grandma told me how important it is to plant trees, and she encouraged me to really think about how we can improve the environment. She was a great teacher who inspired me to dedicate my life to protecting nature.

When I was 10, I went to summer camp in the mountains and was shocked to see that large areas of the pine tree forests were dying because of air pollution. I vowed then and there to help protect the environment.

I kept my promise. Today as a conservationist, I work to protect and restore the environment for wildlife. Specifically, I work to help giant pandas. The biggest threat to giant pandas is the loss of their habitat, the forests where they live. Because of this habitat loss, the wild giant panda population has been shrinking. Even though hundreds of pandas have been born through the captive breeding programs, giant pandas in the wild are still in danger of dying out, or becoming extinct.

To address the increasing threats to giant panda habitat, I created an organization

MARC IN A PANDA SUIT, HAVING FUN AT A PANDA REINTRODUCTION CENTER

called Panda Mountain, which trains people to restore land that has been degraded, or destroyed, by human activity. Working to restore and protect giant panda habitat will benefit wild pandas, conserve biodiversity, and teach us how to care for endangered species. Panda Mountain works to inspire hope and to show how people can change the environment for the better—not just in China but across the entire world. If it's possible to bring the giant panda back from the edge of extinction, then there is hope for other animals as well.

Giant pandas are amazing! I'm thankful that my career allows me to work in the beautiful mountains of central China and help the giant pandas and the other wonderful creatures that live there. Look for me throughout the book as we explore the world of giant pandas.

—Marc Brody

A GIANT PANDA EATS
BAMBOO IN THE FOREST.

CHAPTER 1

A BEAR LIKE NO OTHER

INTRODUCTION

NOT MANY PEOPLE CAN SAY THAT THEY'VE FED, HELD, OR PLAYED WITH A PANDA CUB.

But along with my son, Nate, and my daughter, Louisa, I got to do exactly that—with *eight* panda cubs. It was an experience we'll all remember for the rest of our lives.

MARC BRODY

Once when Nate was busy with one panda, another frisky cub climbed onto his back and gave him a playful nibble. Nate yelped in surprise, but he wasn't hurt. We still laugh about that playful panda.

The love of pandas is something people around the world share. I'm continually amazed by how pandas delight people of all ages and how pandas can put huge bright smiles on the faces of so many.

Even after 20 years of working to help pandas, I still feel excitement and joy when I'm around them! Everyone's efforts to preserve and restore the panda's beautiful habitat are critical to helping them. Saving panda habitat will increase the wild population of our beloved friend and the other wonderful wildlife that share the panda's unique mountain environment.

While pandas are adorable and comical, they also teach us valuable life lessons. You don't see pandas in a rush or in a tizzy.

Pandas work hard to take care of the basics—it's super fun to watch them chomp on bamboo and chill out, or snooze in funny positions. They definitely specialize in taking it easy. But giant pandas represent more than just fun and relaxation.

Since ancient times, these bears have been known to possess a rare combination of characteristics. They are powerful and ferocious when necessary, but they prefer peace and solitude.

By possessing opposite traits, including contrasting black-and-white markings, pandas embody the Chinese and Taoist principle of yin and yang. This is the idea that opposite forces complement, or balance, each other.

I'm hopeful that the public's love for pandas will inspire people to take action to save their habitat and maintain a needed balance between our modern lives and nature.

With the giant panda's blend of unique physical attributes and lovable characteristics, it's easy to see how this special bear became an ambassador, a symbol for wildlife protection, and one of China's national treasures.

MARC AND HIS SON, NATE, HAVING FUN WITH GIANT PANDA CUBS

I'M HOPEFUL THAT THE PUBLIC'S LOVE FOR PANDAS WILL INSPIRE PEOPLE TO TAKE ACTION TO SAVE THEIR HABITAT.

MARC SHARES A PLAYFUL MOMENT WITH HIS DAUGHTER, LOUISA, AND A PANDA CUB.

HIGH IN THE COOL, MISTY MOUNTAINS OF CENTRAL CHINA GROW FORESTS OF TOWERING BAMBOO.

It's funny that they're called forests, because bamboo isn't a tree. Bamboo is actually a type of grass.

STRONG JAWS HELP THE PANDA BITE THROUGH TOUGH BAMBOO.

THE GIANT PANDA IS A NATIONAL TREASURE AND SYMBOL OF PEACE, STRENGTH, AND FRIENDSHIP.

A National Treasure

Grasses, including bamboo, are not very nutritious, but one animal spends much of its day munching on their green leaves and stems. That animal is the giant panda. One look at these black-and-white animals, and you can tell that they're special. They're so special, in fact, that giant pandas have come to symbolize China, and China considers the giant panda its national treasure.

To the people of China, the giant panda is a symbol of strength, peace, and friendship. Its black-and-white coloring represents yin and yang. This ancient Chinese theory describes a universe that stays balanced by opposites such as good and evil, light and dark, male and female, and black and white. The yin and yang symbol itself is black and white.

THE BLACK-AND-WHITE YIN AND YANG SYMBOL REPRESENTS A BALANCE OF OPPOSITES.

A Treasure in Trouble

Even with all that the giant panda represents, this national treasure is in trouble. Pandas have roamed the continent of Asia for millions of years, but more recently humans have begun to move into their habitat. Scientists believe that in prehistoric times, the panda's habitat may have covered most of eastern, central, and southern China. Its home range probably stretched as far south as Myanmar (formerly known as Burma) and as far north as Beijing, China (see page 105). The hundreds of thousands of square miles of giant panda habitat were once all connected. But today, its habitat is much smaller and is broken up by roads, farms, and houses.

At one time, there were an estimated 100,000 giant pandas. Now surveys show fewer than 2,000 giant pandas roam the bamboo forests that are

GIANT PANDAS LIVE IN CHINA'S MOUNTAINOUS BAMBOO FORESTS.

scattered in the mountains of central China. Two thousand is a low number, but it used to be worse. In the mid-1960s, the giant panda was listed on the International Union for Conservation of Nature's (IUCN) Red List of Threatened Species and was considered "very rare." The actual number of giant pandas wasn't tracked until the 1970s, after China had already put aside land to help increase their population. The first official survey was conducted from 1974 to 1977 and estimated there to be 2,459 giant pandas. By the time the second survey came around in the mid-1980s, the number had dropped to 1,216. And by 1990, the giant panda's status was changed to "endangered." The third survey took place from 2000 to 2004 and estimated that the giant panda population had increased to 1,596. In 2016, the giant panda population was estimated to be a little higher at 1,864, and the panda's status changed to "vulnerable." Because of its history of near extinction, and of course, its cuteness factor, the giant panda has become a symbol of animal conservation around the world.

THE RED LIST

THE IUCN RED LIST OF THREATENED SPECIES first started identifying plants and animals that were in danger of dying out in 1964. At that time, scientists hadn't yet developed scientific ways to gather information on species population or habitat health, two important factors that determine how a species is categorized on the Red List. Instead, they got most of their information from stories told by explorers and big-game hunters. Today, the IUCN has strict methods for determining species population and habitat health. Below is its list of categories for threatened animals in the wild.

EXTINCTION RISK →

- EXTINCT (EX)
- EXTINCT IN THE WILD (EW)
- CRITICALLY ENDANGERED (CR)
- ENDANGERED (EN)
- VULNERABLE (VU)
- NEAR THREATENED (NT)
- LEAST CONCERN (LC)

FAME FOR A CAUSE

THE WORLD WILDLIFE FUND (WWF) is a wildlife conservation organization that was founded in 1961. At that time, the Chinese government needed help with conservation issues such as saving and protecting land, plants, and animals, so it turned to the WWF.

It just so happened that a panda named Chi-Chi had been moved to the London Zoo and was getting a lot of media attention. The WWF needed a strong logo that people around the world would recognize and understand. A giant panda like Chi-Chi seemed the perfect choice. The WWF logo has turned a spotlight on the giant panda, and other endangered wildlife, and has helped this charming animal become one of the most recognized symbols of wildlife conservation.

CHI-CHI THE GIANT PANDA AT THE LONDON ZOO

Legendary Bears

The giant panda has been part of the Chinese people's history and writings for thousands of years. Sima Qian, a Chinese historian who lived during the Han dynasty, more than 2,000 years ago, wrote of a tribe that tamed wild animals and used them to defeat another clan. The group of animals described in the story includes tigers, leopards, bears, and giant pandas. The warriors called the giant panda *pixiu* and thought it a fierce animal as strong as a tiger. The pixiu symbolized victory in war.

In the book *The Classic of Mountains and Seas,* a compilation of Chinese mythology written around 2,700 years ago, giant pandas were described as black-and-white bears. They were also called iron-eating bears by people who thought that the panda's wide, flat molars (back teeth) were strong enough to chew through metal. Some said they saw giant pandas eating cooking utensils made of iron or copper. Were they actually eating the metal? It's more likely they were trying to eat the bamboo handles and bindings that were attached to the metal pots of that time.

In the Western Jin dynasty about a thousand years later, the giant panda was called *zhouya,* which referred to a more peaceful creature. It was said that carrying a flag with the word "zhouya" written on it would stop a battle. That's because the zhouya was the

A PAINTED PORTRAIT OF SIMA QIAN

THROUGHOUT HISTORY, GIANT PANDAS HAVE BEEN GIVEN MANY NICKNAMES, INCLUDING *ZHU XIONG,* WHICH MEANS "BAMBOO BEAR."

symbol of friendship and peace.

Throughout time, people from various regions in China have come up with other pet names for giant pandas. The names are often based on the panda's appearance or living habits. For instance, one nickname is *bai xiong,* which means "white bear," and another is *zhu xiong,* which means "bamboo bear." They have also been called Chinese bear, flowery-bear, and *mo.* The official Chinese name for the giant panda, though, is *da xióng māo.*

During much of the Ming dynasty, people respected and admired the giant panda. When the book titled *Compendium of Materia Medica* was written by Li Shizhen in the 1500s, the author wrote that giant pandas also had healing properties for humans. This book, which describes Chinese herbal remedies, advised that sleeping on giant panda fur would keep a person from becoming cold and wet. It would also protect the person from lice and other bugs. And if you were worried about tumors, you could rub oil made of panda fat on your skin to prevent them from forming.

Because of these beliefs, giant pandas were widely hunted for their fur and oil. Today, there are strict laws in China that make it illegal to hunt giant pandas for any reason.

Considering their importance to the Chinese people, it's no wonder that the mystery and admiration surrounding giant pandas would inspire folktales. Even the ancient Tibetan people, who might have glimpsed these bears in their mountains, had a folktale about how giant pandas got their colors. Although many versions of this folktale have been passed down through the years, the story goes something like this:

A long time ago, pure-white giant pandas lived high in the mountains of Tibet. Not a speck of black could be found on their fur. Every day, four shepherdesses would watch their flocks of sheep in a valley at the edge of the forest. And every day, the giant pandas would join them for play. The pandas and the shepherdesses became great friends.

One day, the shepherdesses were playing with a little panda cub when, suddenly, a leopard leaped out of the forest to attack the cub. The shepherdesses could not let their friend die, so they threw themselves in front of the cub. They saved the cub, but all four of the shepherdesses were killed by the leopard.

When word of this tragedy reached the giant pandas, they were heartbroken. But they were so grateful that the little panda cub was saved that they decided to honor the shepherdesses with a memorial service. As was the custom at the time, the giant pandas spread black ashes on their arms. They wept with grief and wiped the tears away with their paws. The ash blackened their eyes. The sound of crying became so loud that the giant pandas had to cover their ears. The ash turned their ears black. And they all needed soothing, so they hugged one another, leaving black ash on their bodies.

Folktales such as this one are stories or legends passed down from person to person through the centuries. They're a fun way of explaining some of the mysteries in life, like how and why pandas are black and white.

Black-and-White Teddy Bear

With their big round heads, roly-poly bodies, and thick fur, it's not surprising that giant pandas are members of the bear family. They look like huggable teddy bears, and they're even called panda bears by some people. But for a long time, scientists weren't completely sure that giant pandas were actually bears.

The first time a giant panda was noticed by anyone outside of China was in 1869. The natural history museum in Paris sent priest and zoologist Armand David to China to collect plants and animals that were unknown to Parisians of that time. He saw a giant panda pelt and thought it was so pretty that he brought one back to Paris. A zoologist at the natural history museum named the new species *Ailuropoda melanoleuca,*

AT FIRST, SOME SCIENTISTS THOUGHT GIANT PANDAS WERE A TYPE OF CAT.

CATS HAVE VERTICAL PUPILS LIKE GIANT PANDAS.

SCIENTISTS ALSO WONDERED IF GIANT PANDAS WERE RELATED TO RACCOONS.

which translated word for word means "cat foot, black and white."

"Cat foot?" Where did that come from? After Armand David brought the giant panda skin to France, people couldn't decide whether the giant panda was a bear, a cat, or a raccoon. Although the reason for calling the giant panda "cat foot" seems to have been lost to history, the Chinese name for this bear, *da xióng māo,* means "giant bear cat." But it's the giant panda's eyes, not its feet, that are similar to a cat's. The pupils of both cats and pandas (and a number of other animals) are vertical rather than round. Vertical pupils help nocturnal animals, those that are active at night, see in the dark. Vertical pupils are also better than round pupils at judging distances. Pandas aren't nocturnal, but they do have three times of day that they're active: morning, afternoon, and midnight. Those vertical pupils come in handy when pandas are awake in the dark of night.

But why did some people think giant pandas are a type of raccoon? Shortly after Armand David brought his panda pelt to France, another French scientist decided that the bone structure of giant pandas is like that of red pandas, a catlike animal that had been in the raccoon family, Procyonidae, at that time. More recently, red pandas have been classified in the family Ailuridae, which they share only with some extinct species. But scientists have discovered that instead of having a common ancestor, giant and red pandas developed similar features because they evolved in similar habitats and ate the same food—bamboo.

To find out once and for all which family giant pandas belong to, scientists studied the panda's DNA. DNA is short for

GIANT PANDAS HAVE VERTICAL PUPILS— SIMILAR TO THE PUPILS OF THIS SLOW LORIS.

DESPITE THE NAME, RED PANDAS ARE NOT RELATED TO GIANT PANDAS.

17

RED PANDAS ARE RELATIVES OF WEASELS, SKUNKS, AND RACCOONS, AND ARE CLOSER TO THE SIZE OF A RACCOON THAN TO THAT OF A BEAR.

RED PANDAS ARE KNOWN FOR THEIR LONG STRIPED TAIL.

RED PANDAS GET THEIR COMMON NAME FROM THE RED COLOR OF THEIR FUR.

THE FIRE-COLORED CAT

GIANT PANDAS WERE NOT THE FIRST animals to be given the name "panda." That honor belongs to the red panda. The giant panda is called "giant" because it's bigger than the red panda, but no one knows for sure how they both came to be called "panda." Some scientists believe the name "panda" came from the Nepalese word for panda, *nigalya ponya,* which translates to "bamboo footed."

In 1825, 44 years before Armand David brought a giant panda pelt from China, French zoologist Frédéric Cuvier was the first to give the red panda its scientific name. He thought it was such a beautiful animal that he named it *Ailurus fulgens,* which means "fire-colored cat." It is thought that Cuvier called red pandas "cats"

because they are small and have a long tail. Red pandas get their common name from the red color of their fur.

The red panda, also called the lesser panda, may share a name with the giant panda, but the two animals are quite different. For starters, red pandas have pointed ears and a long tail, whereas giant pandas have rounded ears and stubby tails. Most important, though, is that red pandas are not bears. They are relatives of weasels, skunks, and raccoons, and are closer to the size of a raccoon than to that of a bear.

Red pandas typically live alone, but once in a while they do live in families or in even bigger groups. They are found mostly in the forests of central China, Nepal, India, Myanmar, and Bhutan.

deoxyribonucleic acid, and it partly controls the characteristics of all living beings. The color of your eyes and hair, whether you will be tall or short, and even if you will eventually need glasses are all determined by your DNA. And because DNA is passed down from parents to child, DNA can show whether individuals are related. So scientists decided to compare the giant panda's DNA with that of the two different types of animals. Giant pandas were thought to be bears or raccoons. Many more matches were found between the DNA of giant pandas and bears than between giant pandas and raccoons. These results were enough to convince scientists that the giant panda belongs to the bear family, known in the scientific world as Ursidae.

FAMILY RESEMBLANCE, LIKE WE SEE WITH THESE SISTERS, CAN BE AN INDICATION OF SHARED DNA.

Living Fossils

Scientists believe that the giant panda's ancestors have been in the Ursidae family for about 30 million years. Between 18 and 25 million years ago, these ancestors began to change and grow into separate species.

The 11-million-year-old *Kretzoiarctos beatrix* is the oldest giant panda relative that has been recorded. It even climbed trees and ate tough-to-chew plants like bamboo. Finding a new type of ancient animal is always exciting and surprising. But one of the most interesting aspects of the 2012 discovery of a *Kretzoiarctos beatrix* jaw is that it was found in Spain—not in Asia. Fossils of this ancient panda relative have not been found outside of Spain, so no one knows whether *Kretzoiarctos beatrix* ever

made it to China. But some of its descendants migrated to eventually reach Asia.

A small bear named *Ailurarctos lufengensis* lived about eight million years ago. Scientists found this clue to the panda's family tree when they discovered the bear's fossilized teeth in Yunnan, a province in central China. They were similar to the giant panda's bamboo-crushing molars.

The skull of an *Ailuropoda microta,* another ancient giant panda, was found in a cave in Guangxi, southern China. *Ailuropoda microta* lived between 2 and 2.4 million years ago, and scientists describe it as being about half the size of today's giant pandas. The shape of the skull, its flat molars, and its heavy jaw muscles are signs that *Ailuropoda microta* was probably already eating mostly bamboo. Scientists even found wear marks on the teeth where these giant panda ancestors probably ground down bamboo stalks.

Except for doubling in size, the giant panda has hardly changed at all in the past two million years. Giant pandas are living fossils!

AN ARTIST'S ILLUSTRATION OF *KRETZOIARCTOS BEATRIX*

A KINGDOM OF SPECIES

MILLIONS OF PLANT AND ANIMAL SPECIES LIVE ON OUR PLANET. And people, being the brainiacs that we are, have tried to organize and make sense of all these critters and plants for centuries.

At first, early people probably organized plants and animals into two groups: those that are helpful to us and those that harm us. Then in the fourth century B.C., the Greek philosopher Aristotle came up with his own ideas. He divided living things into two groups: plants and animals. He then divided animals into those that had blood and those that didn't. And finally, he put animals into one of three groups depending on how they got around on Earth: by swimming, walking, or flying. This organization was used until Carolus Linnaeus came along in the 18th century.

CAROLUS LINNAEUS, SWEDISH NATURALIST

Linnaeus was a scientist from Sweden, and he had some royal ideas. He divided all of nature into one of three kingdoms, either the plant kingdom, the animal kingdom, or minerals. He further divided the kingdoms into smaller groups that allow us to identify a species with a two-part name. This two-part name tells us how the species is related to other species. Here's how it works:

Each organism is placed into smaller groups according to its phylum, class, order, family, genus, and species. Let's look at human beings as an example.

We belong to the phylum Chordata, the class Mammalia, the order Primates, the family Hominidae, the genus *Homo,* and the species *sapiens.* The genus and species names are put together to form the two-part species name. For humans, this name is *Homo sapiens.*

Giant pandas belong to the phylum Chordata, the class Mammalia, the order Carnivora, the family Ursidae, the genus *Ailuropoda,* and the species *melanoleuca.* The giant panda's two-part name is *Ailuropoda melanoleuca.* Did you notice that pandas are in the same phylum and class as humans? That's because we both have spines, so we both belong in the Chordata phylum, and we're both mammals.

This classification system, also called taxonomy, shows us how all of nature is connected. It illustrates how plants and animals have evolved since the beginning of time. But maybe most importantly, it gives us a handy way to identify and talk about different organisms.

As you can see, scientists identify a particular type of plant or animal by its genus and species names, much like you are identified by your first and last names. But unlike your full name, only the genus name is capitalized. Both genus and species names are written in italics.

You may be wondering why names are so important. We've already seen the confusion that the common names "giant panda" and "red panda" have caused. But when you look at their scientific names, *Ailuropoda melanoleuca* for the giant panda and *Ailurus fulgens* for the red panda, all confusion is cleared. Scientific names help us know a plant or animal's true identity. Scientific names also help people communicate across a variety of languages. A giant panda in French is *panda géant.* In German, a giant panda is *riesenpanda.* But everywhere in the world, the scientific name for a giant panda is *Ailuropoda melanoleuca.*

TAXONOMY OF THE GIANT PANDA

KINGDOM ANIMALIA (ANIMALS)

PHYLUM CHORDATA (ANIMALS WITH SPINES)

CLASS MAMMALIA (ANIMALS WITH SPINES AND ARE MAMMALS)

ORDER CARNIVORA (ANIMALS WITH SPINES, ARE MAMMALS, AND PRIMARILY EAT MEAT)

FAMILY URSIDAE (ANIMALS WITH SPINES, ARE MAMMALS, PRIMARILY EAT MEAT, AND ARE BEARS)

GENUS AILUROPODA (ANIMALS WITH SPINES, ARE MAMMALS, PRIMARILY EAT MEAT, ARE BEARS, AND ARE A TYPE OF PANDA)

SPECIES MELANOLEUCA (ANIMALS WITH SPINES, ARE MAMMALS, PRIMARILY EAT MEAT, ARE BEARS, ARE A TYPE OF PANDA, AND IS A GIANT PANDA)

Makeup of a Mammal

What do people, whales, dogs, elephants, bats, and giant pandas all have in common? We're all mammals. Yes, even whales and bats are mammals. How can that be when we're so different?

Whales swim in the ocean and bats fly, but people, dogs, elephants, and giant pandas all walk on land. So then, what makes us all mammals?

Well, hair, for one. Or fur. Really, there is no difference between hair and fur other than who's wearing it. People have hair, while animals have fur. Either way, though, hairy, furry creatures are mammals. Even whales have a bit of fur, although some have it only when they're babies. And even though bats fly, they have fur, not feathers. With their black-and-white fuzziness, there's no denying that giant pandas have fur.

What else makes mammals different from other animals such as birds, fish, reptiles, and amphibians? All female mammals produce milk from their body to feed their babies, and all mammals are warm-blooded. That means we can regulate our own body heat. Not every mammal regulates its heat in the same way, though. People jump up and down and shiver to stay warm, and we sweat when we get hot. Giant pandas release heat from their bodies by panting like dogs do.

PANDAS RELEASE HEAT FROM THEIR BODIES BY PANTING—JUST LIKE DOGS!

WHISKERS

ALL MAMMALS HAVE HAIR OR FUR, EVEN SEA MAMMALS LIKE THIS BOTTLENOSE DOLPHIN!

MAMMALS PRODUCE MILK TO FEED THEIR BABIES.

And giant pandas have a thick coat of fur to keep them warm. They also migrate to the warmer lowlands if it gets too cold for them in the mountains (and if their habitat spans both regions).

All mammals are vertebrates, which means they have a backbone, or spine. The spine is a series of bones, and each of these bones is called a vertebra. You can feel your spine by running your hand up and down the middle of your back. One of the jobs the spine has is to help support the body. Fish, reptiles, amphibians, and birds have spines and are vertebrates, too. But they all lack at least one of the other traits needed to be called a mammal.

GIANT PANDAS HAVE A VERTICAL SPINE LIKE THAT OF HUMANS' OR GORILLAS'.

For instance, they don't have fur or produce milk for their babies.

Most mammals walk on four legs and have a horizontal spine. A giant panda's spine is shaped a bit differently than that of most other mammals. It's vertical, more like a gorilla's or a human's spine. A vertical spine allows people and gorillas to stand up on their hind legs. But giant pandas don't stand for more than a few seconds. So why do they have a vertically oriented spine? They sit upright when they eat. And they eat for most of the day.

It makes sense that their spine would develop in a way similar to other animals that have an upright posture.

A GIANT PANDA'S VERTICAL SPINE ALLOWS IT TO SIT UPRIGHT.

Traits Giant Pandas Share With Other Bears

Bears are big, strong, and sometimes scary-looking animals. They're mostly shy, but they will attack if they or their cubs are threatened. Most bears live alone, although some bear cubs stay with their mom for two to three years.

Bears live in the wild in North and South America, Asia, and Europe. (Africa used to be part of this list, but the Atlas bear became extinct in the 1870s.) But what about koala bears? Despite their name, koala bears—famous for living in Australia—are not bears. Like kangaroos, they are marsupials, a special group of mammals that carry their young in a pouch.

The Ursidae family includes eight bear species: American black bear, Asiatic black bear, brown bear, polar bear, sloth bear, spectacled bear, sun bear, and of course, the giant panda. You may be wondering what happened to the grizzly bear. Grizzly bears are a subspecies of the brown bear. Many other subspecies of bears are lumbering around the world as well.

THE FLAT MOLARS IN THE BACK OF THE PANDA'S MOUTH ARE GOOD FOR CHOMPING ON BAMBOO.

THE KOALA IS NOT A BEAR.

Although the eight species of bears might look slightly different from one another and live in different environments and have varied traits, they also have a lot in common. For instance, most bears are large and have stocky, chunky-looking bodies.

Giant pandas share some more traits with other bears. As adults they don't have to watch out for other predators, and they have to protect their young. Bears walk with their feet flat on the ground, whereas most other animals walk on their toes. And bears have large flat molars that are perfect for chomping on plants and other vegetation.

The giant panda is different from the other bear species in many ways, though. Most bears can stand up on their two hind legs for long periods. Not giant pandas. They can do this for only a short while. Maybe that's because a giant panda's hind legs are small compared to those of other bears. Many members of the Ursidae family have long, sharp claws that they use for digging and ripping apart logs as they look for food. But giant pandas use their claws to help them climb trees.

Another way that giant pandas are different from other bears is that most bears are omnivores, which means they eat plants and animals. But most of a giant panda's diet is made up of bamboo. Giant pandas don't roar like other bears, either—instead, a panda bleats like a sheep, barks and growls like a dog, squeaks, and even makes huffing sounds. The most noticeable difference between a giant panda and other bears, though, is the panda's unique black-and-white markings.

BROWN BEAR CUBS STAY WITH THEIR MOM FOR TWO TO THREE YEARS.

MANY BEARS, LIKE THIS BROWN BEAR, HAVE LONG CLAWS FOR DIGGING INSECTS OUT OF LOGS.

THE BARE FACTS ABOUT BEARS

LET'S LEARN A BIT ABOUT the eight bear species that make up the Ursidae family.

SUN BEAR

SCIENTIFIC NAME: *Helarctos malayanus*
SIZE: 4 to 5 feet (1.2–1.5 m) long
WEIGHT: 60–150 pounds (27–68 kg)
RANGE: China, India, and Indonesia
AVERAGE LIFE SPAN: Up to 25 years in the wild
FUN FACT: Mother sun bears sometimes walk on their hind legs, carrying their babies in their arms.

BROWN BEAR

SCIENTIFIC NAME: *Ursus arctos*
SIZE: 4.6 to 9.2 feet (1.4–2.8 m) long
WEIGHT: 800 pounds (363 kg)
RANGE: Central and southern Asia, Russia, Japan, and the mountains of northern North America
AVERAGE LIFE SPAN: 25 years in the wild
FUN FACT: Brown bears live in more places in the world than any other bear.

SPECTACLED BEAR

SCIENTIFIC NAME: *Tremarctos ornatus*
SIZE: 5 to 6 feet (1.5–1.8 m) long
WEIGHT: 220 to 340 pounds (100–154 kg)
RANGE: Andean jungles of South America
AVERAGE LIFE SPAN: 25 years in captivity; unknown in the wild
FUN FACT: They're called "spectacled" because these bears have rings around their eyes that make it look like they are wearing glasses.

GIANT PANDA

SCIENTIFIC NAME: *Ailuropoda melanoleuca*
SIZE: 5 to 6 feet (1.5–1.8 m) long
WEIGHT: 165 to 300 pounds (75–136 kg)
RANGE: Mountain forests of central China
AVERAGE LIFE SPAN: 20 years in the wild
FUN FACT: Panda babies are the smallest newborn mammal compared to the size of the mother.

SLOTH BEAR

SCIENTIFIC NAME: *Melurus ursinus*
SIZE: 5 to 6 feet (1.5–1.8 m) long
WEIGHT: 120 to 310 pounds (54–141 kg)
RANGE: India, Nepal, Bangladesh, and Sri Lanka
AVERAGE LIFE SPAN: Thought to be around 20 years in the wild
FUN FACT: Sloth bears are the only bears that carry their babies on their backs.

AMERICAN BLACK BEAR

SCIENTIFIC NAME: *Ursus americanus*
SIZE: 5 to 6 feet (1.5–1.8 m) long
WEIGHT: 200 to 600 pounds (91–272 kg)
RANGE: North America
AVERAGE LIFE SPAN: 20 years in the wild
FUN FACT: American black bears aren't always black. They come in shades of gray, black, and brown, and sometimes white.

ASIATIC BLACK BEAR

SCIENTIFIC NAME: *Ursus thibetanus*
SIZE: 4 to 6.3 feet (1.2–1.9 m) long
WEIGHT: 200 to 250 pounds (91–113 kg)
RANGE: Central and southern Asia, Russia, and Japan
AVERAGE LIFE SPAN: 15–25 years in the wild
FUN FACT: These bears are also called moon bears because of the sliver of white on their chest that looks somewhat like a crescent moon.

POLAR BEAR

SCIENTIFIC NAME: *Ursus maritimus*
SIZE: 7.3 to 8.0 feet (2.2–2.4 m) long
WEIGHT: 900 to 1,600 pounds (408–726 kg)
RANGE: the Arctic
AVERAGE LIFE SPAN: 25–30 years in the wild
FUN FACT: Each strand of their fur is hollow and reflects all visible light, which is why a polar bear's fur looks white.

THE CASE OF THE BROWN-AND-WHITE PANDAS

THE FIRST RECORDED SIGHTING OF A BROWN-AND-WHITE PANDA was in her home in the Qinling Mountains of central China in the mid-1980s. She was given the name Dan-Dan and was captured to be bred with a male black-and-white panda. Scientists wanted to see if she would give birth to a brown-and-white baby. She didn't. Her cub was the normal black and white of most giant pandas. A few years later, another brown-and-white panda was seen in the wild. She had a black-and-white cub as well.

QIZAI AT SIX YEARS OLD

It wasn't until 2005 that the Qinling panda was established as a subspecies of the giant panda and was given the scientific name *Ailuropoda melanoleuca qinlingensis*. See how there's an extra word, *"qinlingensis,"* in its scientific name? *Qinlingensis* is the Qinling panda's subspecies name. Qinling pandas are like giant pandas in almost every way, but there are a few differences. For instance, Qinling pandas are smaller, have a smaller skull, and are brown and white instead of black and white.

In 2009, a two-month-old brown-and-white giant panda cub was found without his mother, and he was very hungry. He was taken to the Shaanxi Rare Wildlife Rescue and Breeding Research Centre in Shaanxi Province in northwest China and was nursed back to health. The cub was named Qizai, which in Chinese means "seventh son," because he was only the seventh brown-and-white panda seen in the Qinling Mountains within the last 25 years. Qizai currently lives in the Foping Panda Valley and is the only brown-and-white panda in captivity. Some scientists thought that he may be the only brown-and-white giant panda left in the world. But in March of 2018, a brown-and-white panda was caught on camera crossing a stream in the Changqing National Nature Reserve, in Shaanxi Province.

Why are some of these pandas brown and white? One theory has to do with inbreeding. The Qinling panda's habitat is isolated, so pandas from other areas can't wander in. When a population is small, with few or no new members, inbreeding can occur. Inbreeding is when two animals that are closely related mate and have a baby. It can lead to unusual traits. In the case of the Qinling pandas, scientists think that the brown-and-white coloring is an unusual trait brought about by inbreeding.

Black-and-white pandas with patches of brown on their fur have also been seen in the Qinling Mountains area. This makes some scientists think that the change in color may be caused by an unknown environmental factor rather than by inbreeding.

Why Do We Love Pandas?

Look at the picture of a giant panda. It just makes you want to smile. Perhaps your heart melts a little. You want to reach out and pet its soft-looking fur. But if you ever get that chance, don't touch! Giant pandas look gentle and cute, but they are wild animals that have sharp claws and teeth. They should be treated with respect and kept at a distance.

Still, people are drawn to giant pandas. Why? Some scientists think it's because even as adults, giant pandas have a cute, stubby nose, as well as round cheeks and a somewhat toddling walk. This image may trigger that part of our brain that draws us to young children and other baby animals. Baby animals usually have rounder heads than adults, and their eyes are large for their head. The black patches around a giant panda's eyes make them seem larger and make the panda appear more cublike. Giant pandas' antics are a lot like those of human kids: they climb trees, do handstands, and perform somersaults. Who wouldn't love these adorable animals?

Zoos that have giant pandas on display report that thousands of visitors come to see the black-and-white bears every year. And panda cams have hundreds of thousands of viewers online. Regardless of the reason, there's no denying that people love giant pandas.

PANDA CAM!

SOME ZOOS AND RESEARCH INSTITUTIONS have set up webcams in their giant panda exhibits. Ask a grown-up for permission to go online to check out these giant panda webcams:

Chengdu Research Base of Giant Panda Breeding: webcamtaxi.com/en/china/sichuan-province /giant-panda-cam.html

Edinburgh Zoo: edinburghzoo.org.uk/webcams/panda-cam/

Explore Live Cams: explore.org/livecams/panda-bears/china-panda-cam-1

San Diego Zoo: zoo.sandiegozoo.org/cams/panda-cam

Smithsonian's National Zoo: nationalzoo.si.edu/webcams/panda-cam

Zoo Atlanta: zooatlanta.org/panda-cam/

THE SILLY ANTICS OF PANDAS MAKE THEM EVEN MORE LOVABLE.

CAUGHT ON PANDA CAM! ONE OF THE SMITHSONIAN NATIONAL ZOO'S GIANT PANDAS COMFORTABLY LOUNGING ON A LOG.

PANDA-MAZING!

Each bear species has at least one trait that's special to that type of bear. You read about these traits earlier in this chapter. Let's test your bear knowledge! Can you tell which trait belongs to which bear?

A. HAS TINIEST BABIES COMPARED TO THE SIZE OF ITS GIANT MOM.

B. YOU CAN FIND THIS BEAR ON THREE CONTINENTS.

C. THIS BEAR MAY BE BLACK, BROWN, GRAY, OR WHITE.

D. HOLLOW STRANDS OF HAIR MAKE THIS BEAR'S FUR LOOK WHITE.

E. WHEN IT NEEDS TO CARRY ITS CUBS, THIS BEAR MAMA PUTS THEM ON HER BACK.

F. YOU MAY THINK THIS BEAR IS WEARING GLASSES.

G. THIS BEAR WILL SOMETIMES STAND AND CARRY ITS CUBS IN ITS ARMS.

H. THIS BEAR IS ALSO CALLED A MOON BEAR.

3 POLAR BEAR

2 SLOTH BEAR

1 AMERICAN BLACK BEAR

8 BROWN BEAR

4 SUN BEAR

5 GIANT PANDA

7 SPECTACLED BEAR

6 ASIATIC BLACK BEAR

Answer key: 1. c, 2. e, 3. d, 4. g, 5. a, 6. h, 7. f, 8. b

GIANT PANDAS SOMETIMES
GIVE BIRTH TO TWINS, MAKING
FOR A READY PLAYMATE.

CHAPTER 2
GIANT PANDAS FROM HEAD TO TAIL

INTRODUCTION

SEARCHING FOR SIGNS OF GIANT PANDAS IN THE WILD IS EXCITING.

Broken pieces of bamboo, peeled branches, and claw marks in the bark of nearby trees are clear signs that a panda has been hard at work in the area.

MARC BRODY

Kneeling within a bamboo thicket and doing my best to be as quiet as possible, I could feel the sweat running down the sides of my face and back. I was still worn out from the 1,300-foot (396-m) climb up the mountain, but I was excited and alert, listening for any sound in the silent forest. My guide, Chen, had chosen this spot at the center of the Wolong Nature Reserve because the area has a large population of wild giant pandas.

Pandas have a great sense of smell, and Chen quietly indicated our good fortune to be downwind of our viewing area. After 15 minutes, I heard rustling in the distance. The sound grew louder, and my heart started to race. Could I be lucky enough to see a wild panda? But what I saw next was a blur of bright colors, not my dreamed-of black-and-white pattern. Chen started laughing at the false alarm—we had only glimpsed a golden pheasant, which is like a wild chicken with long tail feathers.

Since giant pandas are hard to spot in the wild, scientists try to track down panda traces such as scratches on trees, scat, or paw prints on the ground. As we walked away from our bamboo thicket, Chen pointed out a tree that had clearly been scratched by panda claws. Perhaps the tree served as a boundary marker of the panda's home range.

I started to search for more clues of panda activity. Not knowing where the tree fit within the panda's territory, I decided to be methodical in my search. I made a quick visual survey of the forest, and made a plan to walk off in four directions: north, south, east, and west. On my second try, I spotted bamboo. Some of the bamboo had been broken, some branches had been peeled off, and the ground was littered with shavings. This was a clear sign that a hungry panda with strong paws and powerful jaws had been eating in that spot. A few minutes later, after carefully scanning the ground, I found my first panda scat in the wild.

I didn't see a wild panda that day, and so far I have not been lucky enough to see a panda in the wild. However, being in panda habitat is always exciting for me. And finding traces of panda activity makes me want to work harder to conserve and restore the habitat that giant pandas call home.

THE GOLDEN PHEASANT SHARES THE GIANT PANDA'S HABITAT.

I HEARD RUSTLING IN THE DISTANCE. THE SOUND GREW LOUDER, AND MY HEART STARTED TO RACE. COULD I BE LUCKY ENOUGH TO SEE A WILD PANDA?

WOLONG NATIONAL NATURAL RESERVE

AN ENTRANCE TO THE WOLONG NATURE RESERVE

THE GIANT PANDA IS ONE OF THE MOST RECOGNIZED BEARS ON THE PLANET.

People instantly know that any white bear with black legs, eye patches, and ears, and a black shoulder is a giant panda.

Patchy Pandas

But why did pandas develop their black-and-white coloring? We're not the only ones who wanted the answer to this question. Some scientists at the University of California, Davis, and California State University, Long Beach, wanted to know, too.

When scientists set off to answer a question about an animal, they often study similar traits of animals closely related to it. This was the first challenge these scientists faced. Other mammals, such as zebras and skunks, are black and white, but no other mammal has the same black-and-white pattern as the giant panda. After some head scratching and a lot of discussion, these scientists came up with a plan. They decided to compare the color of each part of the giant panda's body to the coloring of other animals with dark and light patches. Then they tried to figure out why specific parts of the animals' bodies are dark or light. And, eureka! They discovered the answer—two answers,

MAMMALS, LIKE THIS BOBCAT, WITH BLACK-TIPPED EARS TEND TO BE AGGRESSIVE.

actually. It all has to do with camouflage and communication.

Giant pandas live both in white, snowy mountains and in shadowy forests. The bamboo they eat doesn't give them enough protein to get fat enough to sleep away the winter the way other bears that hibernate do, which means they have to be out and about all year long to eat. Their white coloring helps them blend into the white snow. Their black coloring helps them blend into the shadows of the forests. So scientists think the giant panda's coloring allows them to hide and stay safe in both environments.

The giant panda's eyes and ears are probably black for different reasons. Mammals with black on their ears, such as tigers and bobcats, which have black-tipped ears, tend to be aggressive and sometimes fierce. Giant pandas aren't the most aggressive animal, but a potential enemy might take a look at those black ears and run for the hills. They may be a warning sign to stay away.

Eye patches among giant pandas vary in shape and size, so scientists think giant pandas recognize one another by their eye patches. The eye patches may also serve as a defense mechanism. When a giant panda stares down a predator to protect a cub, or to protect its territory, the panda's fur can stand on end, making its eyes look bigger. Bigger-looking eyes make a giant panda seem more fierce or likely to attack. It's just another signal that tells other animals to stay away. If giant pandas don't plan to attack, they do something really cute to appear less threatening. They cover their eyes with their paws as though they're about to play a game of peekaboo.

A PANDA'S WHITE FUR HELPS IT BLEND INTO THE SNOW.

BLACK EARS MAY SIGNAL FIERCENESS OR AGGRESSIVENESS.

BLACK FUR AROUND THE EYES HELP PANDAS RECOGNIZE ONE ANOTHER AND LOOK MORE AGGRESSIVE.

A PANDA'S BLACK FUR HELPS IT BLEND INTO THE DARK SHADOWS OF THE FOREST.

THE PANDA'S LARGE BLACK-AND-WHITE PATTERN HELPS TO KEEP IT SAFE IN ITS HABITAT.

Big and Burly

Other than their color, giant pandas look like typical bears. They have strong, muscular bodies with thick fur. Giant pandas are two to three feet (60 to 90 cm) tall at the shoulder, and they're five to six feet (1.5 to 1.8 m) long from tip of nose to tip of tail. The tail itself is about six inches (15 cm) long, and thick, and fluffy, although it's hard to see under all that fur and chubbiness. The tail is white like the rest of a panda's back end, and it's usually tucked close to the panda's body. Male giant pandas can weigh up to 300 pounds (136 kg), and females weigh less than 220 pounds (100 kg).

As we learned earlier, a giant panda's hind legs are shorter than their forelegs. Pandas rarely stand on their hind legs, and unlike other bears, giant pandas don't walk upright. But their longer, stronger forelegs come in handy when giant pandas hoist themselves up tree branches as they climb.

A giant panda's feet are slightly pigeon-toed, which means they turn inward toward each other. Some scientists think this helps them hold on to a tree while climbing. And although many mammals, such as dogs and cats, walk on their toes, pandas use their whole foot and walk heel to toe like we do. Their pigeon-toed gait is a slow and lumbering walk. They look like they have all the time in the world to get to where they want to be. But giant pandas can and do run for short distances. They can run in spurts as fast as 20 miles an hour (32 km/h). But they don't keep up that pace for very long.

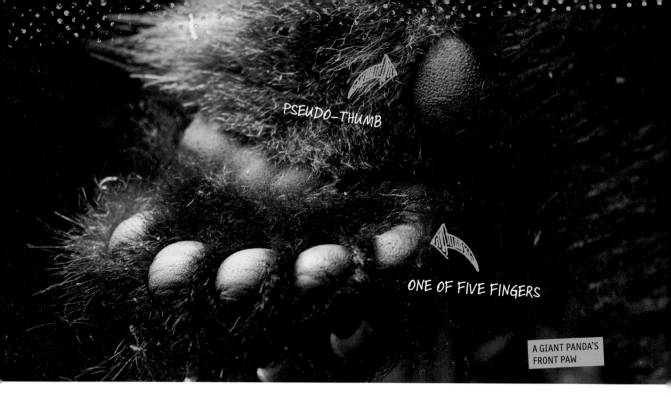

PSEUDO-THUMB

ONE OF FIVE FINGERS

A GIANT PANDA'S FRONT PAW

Fake Thumbs

Like most bears, giant pandas have large paws with five fingers. They walk on their paws, cradle their babies with them, and of course, use them for pulling down stalks of bamboo. Giant pandas eat bamboo the way many of us eat a whole carrot. We use our thumb to help us hold a carrot firmly as we bite into it. But giant pandas don't have thumbs quite like humans. So how do they grab, pull, and hold firmly on to bamboo?

Many parts of a giant panda developed in special ways to help it live in bamboo forests and eat bamboo. Panda paws are no exception. Giant pandas have five toes on their back paws and five fingers on their front paws. But their front paws also have an unusually long wrist bone. This wrist bone is protected by a fleshy pad, as are the fingers and

A RED PANDA USES ITS PSEUDO-THUMB TO GRIP BAMBOO.

toes. But the wrist bone is not topped by a claw as each finger and toe is. The extralong wrist bone acts somewhat like a thumb. In fact, it's called a pseudo-thumb. "Pseudo" means "fake." A panda's real thumb is the finger right next to the pseudo-thumb.

The pseudo-thumb can't move much. It basically acts as a solid surface for the giant panda's true thumb and fingers to squeeze against. The pseudo-thumb and the fingers act like pincers and squeeze together tightly enough to hold objects firmly in place. Pandas need the pseudo-thumb because bamboo stalks are woody and extremely tough. Without the pseudo-thumb's help to hold bamboo tightly, giant pandas wouldn't have the control they need to bite into their food. Red pandas also have pseudo-thumbs, but they mostly eat the bamboo leaves and tender shoots, not the stalks.

TALLY THOSE FOOTPRINTS!

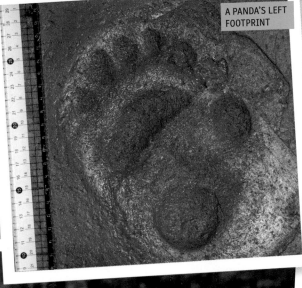

A PANDA'S LEFT FOOTPRINT

WITH THE GIANT PANDA POPULATION SO LOW, it's important to keep count of how many are in the wild. But that's not easy to do. Even though they're rather large, the giant pandas' coloring makes them hard to spot them in their natural habitat. Plus, trekking to the remote areas where pandas live is not easy. But researchers at Duke Kunshan University, in Kunshan, Jiangsu, China, have come up with a way to identify individual pandas, therefore keeping tabs on the giant panda population.

You've heard of identifying criminals by their fingerprints. Now scientists can identify a panda by its footprints. Scientists can get information about the owner of a footprint, including whether the panda is male or female. All that's needed is a photograph of the footprint.

Like human fingerprints, each giant panda's footprint is unique. When a photograph of a panda footprint is entered into ConservationFIT's footprint identification technique (FIT) software, information from the digital image is sent to a global database. The information is compared to data that are already in the system to ensure a giant panda's footprint hasn't already been added to the database. Anyone can take a photo of a panda footprint and submit it to

EACH GIANT PANDA'S FOOTPRINT IS UNIQUE.

ConservationFIT. You just have to follow the steps on the project's website, *conservationfit.org/partner-with-us/*. ConservationFIT has a database for other animal footprints, such as polar bears and tigers, as well. If you want to check out the database for yourself, be sure to get an adult's permission before you go online.

ALL BEARS HAVE RELATIVELY BIG HEADS, BUT THE GIANT PANDA'S IS THE ROUNDEST OF THEM ALL.

A GIANT PANDA HAS 42 TEETH. THE MOLARS IN BACK ARE USED TO GRIND BAMBOO.

A Head for Bamboo

The giant panda's big round head is part of what makes this animal so cute. All bears have relatively big heads, but the giant panda's is the roundest of them all. It needs to be that round to make room for its large and powerful jaws, strong jaw muscles, and large molar teeth. All of these traits developed to make eating bamboo easier for giant pandas.

Take a look inside a giant panda's head and you'll see that this animal has large cranial cavities. Cranial cavities are the spaces inside the skull, or cranium, that a panda's extra thick jaw muscles are attached to. These muscles connect to a giant panda's large jaws, and the result is a strong and powerful bite.

Strong jaw muscles aren't all that's needed to chew the tough stalks of bamboo. Giant pandas also have teeth that are specially made to grind up this woody grass. They have 42 teeth, including canine teeth, which are the longer pointy teeth near the front of the mouth. Most bears use their canine teeth to help them catch and rip at their prey. Giant pandas hardly ever use their canines. Instead, they rely on the broad, flat molars near the back of the mouth to crush and grind tough bamboo.

Taste-Bud Turnabout

Millions of years ago, the giant panda's ancestors ate mainly meat. Today, only the polar bear is a true carnivore, eating only meat. Even though they are classified as carnivores and eat a lot of meat, most bears are actually omnivores. Then you have the giant panda of today, which has a diet that is 99 percent bamboo. Giant pandas are ready-made to handle eating meat, so why did they turn to bamboo as their main food? One theory is that pandas lost the ability to taste meat.

When you take a bite of food, cells in your taste buds called taste receptors tell you whether you have a mouthful of something sweet, bitter, salty, or sour. Giant pandas are able to distinguish flavors, too. In the early 1900s, scientists realized that a fifth flavor exists. They call it umami. This is a flavor that's found in most protein-rich foods such as meat. And although scientists aren't sure when it exactly happened, giant pandas lost the taste receptor for umami sometime in the last few million years. This means meat stopped tasting good to giant pandas, so they turned to the food source that was all around them—bamboo.

Giant pandas had bamboo practically all to themselves. Just a few animals eat bamboo, including gorillas, chimpanzees, elephants, and red pandas. And only the red panda shares the giant panda's habitat. But the red panda is not much competition for the giant panda, since it prefers to eat just the leaf tips and shoots, leaving the other parts of the bamboo for the panda.

GIANT PANDAS MAY HAVE STARTED EATING BAMBOO BECAUSE THEY LOST THE ABILITY TO TASTE MEAT.

Shoots and Leaves on the Menu

All animals need nutrients, most of which they get from the foods they eat. Carbohydrates, fats, proteins, minerals, and vitamins are examples of nutrients. These nutrients supply energy for the animal to grow, hunt, breathe, run—for everything the animal needs to do to stay alive.

Giant pandas get most of their nutrients from bamboo. The plant is not very nutritious, though, so pandas need to eat *a lot* of bamboo to meet their needs. And not all parts of bamboo are created equal. The nutritional goodies in the shoots, leaves, and stems of bamboo can change with the seasons, so pandas eat

different parts of bamboo depending on the time of year. Generally, giant pandas feast on new bamboo growth, called shoots, in the spring. They eat bamboo leaves in the summer and fall, and bamboo stems, called culms, in the winter.

Although 99 percent of a giant panda's diet is bamboo—the other one percent being fruits, vegetables, and a small mammal here and there—the panda has a digestive system that is more like that of a meat-eating carnivore than of a plant-eating herbivore. The giant panda's jaw, teeth, head, and paws developed and adapted to its modern diet, but its digestive system didn't.

After animals chew and swallow their food, the food makes its way through the intestines and gets digested. To digest food, that is, to break it down so the body can use the food's nutrients, special enzymes and bacteria are needed. The giant panda doesn't have enough of the kind of bacteria and enzymes needed to get all the nutrients out of the bamboo. The result is an animal that eats and eats and eats to get the nutrients it needs. Giant pandas spend 10 to 16 hours a day looking for and eating food.

Pandas have responded in other ways to their low-nutrient diet. They move slowly and nap a lot. They don't use much energy, so they won't need as much energy from food. Even though a giant panda's digestive system is not made for eating bamboo, the slow-paced panda has no problem living on a nearly bamboo-only diet.

GIANT PANDAS LOVE TO EAT BAMBOO SHOOTS.

Pass the Bamboo, Please

This is what giant pandas are really good at: passing the bamboo. There's so little nutrition in bamboo that most of it passes right through the panda's body. In fact, giant pandas poop about 50 times a day—they even poop while they're sleeping! That makes sense, since they digest only 17 percent of their food, passing 83 percent out as waste. You can actually see undigested bamboo in panda poop. Because most of what they eat is waste, giant pandas have to eat 20 to 40 pounds (9 to 18 kg) of bamboo a day to make sure they get all the nutrition they need.

Before scientists started using footprints to try to determine the size of the giant panda population, they counted poop. They had to trudge up and down steep mountains and through thick forests in the hopes of catching a glimpse of panda poop. They'd collect the poop and run DNA tests on it to identify the panda. This gave researchers only a rough idea of how many pandas lived in an area partly because the DNA results weren't reliable when tested on old poop. The footprint database has become more cost-effective and reliable because the footprints hold up longer than the poop. But so far no method has been found to accurately count the number of giant pandas in the wild.

Panda poop does have some scientific value, though. By studying the poop, scientists can learn how long it's been since a giant panda was in the area and how much time the panda spent there, as well as the type and parts of the bamboo it was eating. Sometimes they can look at the poop to tell if a giant panda is healthy or sick. Just like people, if the giant panda has runny poop, then it probably had an upset stomach. There are also bugs in the wild called parasites that can infect the digestive system of the giant panda and make it sick. That means scientists can look for evidence of the parasites in the poop see if a panda is infected and might be at risk of getting sick.

UNDIGESTED BAMBOO IS VISIBLE IN PANDA POOP.

A PANDA EATS A LOT OF BAMBOO, AND MUCH OF IT PASSES RIGHT THROUGH ITS BODY IN ITS POOP!

BAMBOO STEMS

Panda Senses

We already know that giant pandas have catlike pupils that are vertical slits, which help them see at night. And although a 2006 study couldn't prove that giant pandas can see in color, it did show that pandas can tell the difference between gray and other colors such as gree reds, and blues.

Their eyesight may not be the best, but giant pandas have an amazing sense of smell. They use scent marking as a way to communicate with each other. The scent may come from urine, or it may come from a bare area under the base of a giant panda's tail. This is where glands that make and release a smelly waxy substance are located. Giant pandas lift their tail and rub the waxy stuff onto surfaces such as trees, tree stumps, bushes, and rocks. Male pandas try to mark their scent as high as they can to show other pandas how big and strong they are. When a male giant panda makes a mark with urine, he may do a handstand to get his mark up as high as possible.

PAPER POOP

A PAPER COMPANY HAS STRUCK A DEAL with giant panda reserves in central China to collect panda poop and other waste. This sounds strange, but the company wants to use panda poo to make luxury facial tissue, toilet paper, and paper towels, and call it Panda Poo.

You might think going from poop to paper doesn't make any sense, but it does! Paper is made from a mixture of fibers. Most of the paper you use comes from the wood fiber of chopped-down trees. In the case of Panda Poo, fiber is the part of the panda's food that doesn't get digested. Fiber has the side effect of making the intestine repeatedly contract, or squeeze, and relax. This helps move food through the body. Eventually, what wasn't digested is released as waste.

The digestion process takes care of some of the paper-making steps by partly breaking down the bamboo fiber. Each adult giant panda passes more than 22 pounds (10 kg) of poop and 110 pounds (50 kg) of chewed-up, spit-out bamboo every day. Now, all this waste isn't going to waste. Don't worry. Panda Poo won't make it into people's homes until it has gone through a 60-step cleaning and recycling process.

PAPER PRODUCTS SUCH AS THESE TISSUES ARE MADE OF PROCESSED PANDA POOP.

A GIANT PANDA RUBS A SMELLY SUBSTANCE ON A BAMBOO WALL.

SCENT MARKING

A GIANT PANDA IS MARKING HIS SCENT HIGH ON A TREE.

Male giant pandas also use their scent to mark their territory. When another panda walks by and gets a whiff, he knows that area is occupied and that he needs to stay out. The passing panda can even tell how long ago the area was marked and whether it was marked by a male or a female. When it's breeding season, a female giant panda's special under-the-tail gland odor tells males that she's ready to mate.

What about panda taste buds? The giant panda's sense of taste has changed over millions of years. We already know that one of the reasons scientists think giant pandas switched from a meat-eating to a bamboo-eating diet is because they lost the ability to taste meat. But scientists have found another difference in taste preferences between giant pandas and other non-bear carnivores: Giant pandas, like most bears, have a sweet tooth. That's not surprising, since they've been caught eating honey and sweet potatoes.

And while everyone knows how cute panda ears are, you might not know that giant pandas' sense of hearing is so good that they can hear high-pitched ultrasonic sounds. These sounds are so high pitched that only some other animals, such as bats and dogs, can hear them. Being able to hear ultrasonic sounds can be good. Bats use these sounds as part of their echolocation to find food. Giant pandas communicate ultrasonically during mating season. Scientists worry that sounds coming from human activities near giant panda habitats could interfere with ultrasonic sound and confuse giant pandas. They're especially worried that human-made noise interferes with the pandas' vocalizations during mating time, therefore hurting their chances of reproduction.

BATS USE ULTRASOUND AND ECHOLOCATION TO FIND THEIR FOOD.

LET'S TRANSLATE PANDA SPEAK!

GIANT PANDAS MAKE A LOT OF SOUNDS, more than any other type of bear. Researchers have identified 13 different ways that pandas express themselves vocally. For solitary animals, animals that prefer to live alone, that's a lot of talking! Some scientists are using voice-recognition technology to try to develop a panda translator. So, what do giant pandas sound like? Well, it depends on what they have to say.

Although the results aren't official (they haven't yet been published and accepted by the scientific community), scientists conducting a study of panda speak at the China Conservation and Research Center for the Giant Panda have put together a Panda-English dictionary of sorts. Giant pandas start "talking" when they're little cubs. They learn to bark, bleat, chirp, shout, and squeak. But pandas don't roar the way other bears do. Here are the meanings behind some panda speak:

WOW-WOW
"I'm sad," or "Stop bothering me."

MOAN
General sound made when walking around or falling asleep. A moaning panda sounds similar to a Wookiee from *Star Wars*.

SQUEAL
General cub sound

BLEAT (*BAA,* LIKE A SHEEP)
"I'm ready to mate!" (male panda calling out to female panda) or "I'm hungry! Give me something!" or "Come here, children!" (mother panda calling out to her cubs)

GEE-GEE
"I'm hungry!" or "More, please."

HONK OR HICCUP
"I feel stressed."

COO-COO
"Nice!"

BARK
"Go away!"

TWEET/CHIRP
"I'm worried about my babies," or "I'm ready to mate!" (female panda calling out to male panda)

GET A GROWN-UP'S PERMISSION TO GO ONLINE to hear what giant pandas actually sound like at *pdxwildlife.com/sounds-pandas-make/*.

A MOTHER PANDA AND HER CUB REST IN THEIR DEN INSIDE A HOLLOW LOG.

Acrobats in the Trees

Bamboo isn't the only tall plant that grows in a bamboo forest. Trees grow there, too. It's a good thing that they do because the only way to get to the delicious leaves high up on the bamboo is to climb a nearby tree.

Giant pandas might look awkward when they walk around on the ground, but they are excellent tree climbers. Their thick, sharp claws are perfect for climbing. And climbing trees helps pandas keep their claws trimmed. Surprisingly for such lumbering animals, giant pandas are perfectly comfortable up high in tree branches. They can even be downright nimble, moving easily from branch to branch.

In addition to climbing trees to reach the tops of taller bamboo, giant pandas use trees as

YOUNG PANDAS CLIMB TREES TO ESCAPE PREDATORS.

a safe place to escape from danger. Starting at the age of five months, a young panda can flee from predators by scampering up a tree. It might spend hours among the branches before feeling safe enough to come down. And hanging out high up in a tree isn't so bad, because pandas have fun playing among the branches. A panda can swing from branch to branch, hang from tree limbs—sometimes upside down—and even walk from tree to tree on branches. And somehow, pandas can make themselves comfortable enough to get a good nap up high in a tree. They usually sleep for two to four hours at a time between stretches of eating.

Female giant pandas also use the hollow logs and stumps of dead trees as dens, where they raise their cubs. Most dens are roomy

PANDA CLAW MARKS

A PANDA CLAWED THIS TREE TO MARK ITS TERRITORY.

PANDAS CAN EVEN NAP IN TREES.

inside, but their entrance is small, which keeps the den warm.

Alone in the Woods

Giant pandas live 5,000 to 10,000 feet (1,525 to 3,050 m) high in the damp forest mountains of central China. They are mostly shy and solitary animals, preferring to be alone munching on bamboo than frolicking about with other pandas. When two giant pandas encounter each other, they may squat or growl, and maybe even try to bite each other.

Just as difficult as it is to determine the size of the giant panda population, it's difficult to determine a giant panda's home range. But one study estimates

PANDAS ARE MOSTLY SOLITARY AND PREFER TO BE ALONE LOOKING FOR AND MUNCHING ON BAMBOO.

that a giant panda claims a territory that averages about 2.3 square miles (6 sq km), with males tending to have a larger territory than females. Along with urine and scent marking, giant pandas leave claw marks on trees to mark their territory.

As much as giant pandas prefer to be alone, researchers have discovered that pandas may form loose groups of about 7 to 15 animals. They're "loose" groups because each panda maintains its own territory, although it may be right next to or overlap another's territory. Individuals in a group socialize with one another. As mentioned, they may play together in tree branches, and they may mate with one another. Scientists have noticed, though, that for the most part, pandas from different groups tend to avoid each other.

Getting Ready for Baby

Female giant pandas need to be between four and six years old before they can start having cubs. And they can continue reproducing until they're about 20. In the wild, giant pandas mate in the spring, between February and June. Each female panda has a two- to three-day time period when she can become pregnant. She shows her readiness by scent marking on rocks and trees with her special odor. This is the noisiest time of year for giant pandas, because males and females are vocalizing a lot.

A female panda that is ready to mate stays in a tree while a few males fight over the privilege of mating with her. They bark and wrestle with one another, lunging and swatting, until one is the winner. Then he stands guard at the base of the tree, chasing away any other males that come by. He has to wait until the

female decides to come down from the tree. Then they mate. But giant panda pregnancy is special. If mating is successful, the female panda may be pregnant, but her fertilized egg might not grow—at least not yet.

With most mammals, the fertilized egg attaches, or implants, to the mother nearly right away. The fertilized egg of a giant panda starts to grow, but then scientists think it stops growing, and that it doesn't grow again until it attaches to the mother several weeks before birth. This is called delayed implantation. A few other mammals, including skunks and kangaroos, go through delayed implantation, too. Scientists aren't sure why this happens, but one reason might be to make sure the baby is born when the mother will have enough food to produce the milk she would need to feed her cub. Because of this delayed implantation, a female panda gives birth from three to six months after mating. Whether their implantation as an egg was delayed or not, all cubs are born at the same stage of development—tiny, helpless, and nearly hairless.

Before giving birth, though, the mother-to-be searches for a safe place to make her den, such as a hollow tree. She forms a tiny nest of branches and dry grass for her newborn. As the cub's birth gets closer, the mother panda spends more time in her den.

One reason the giant panda population is growing so slowly is that female pandas can give birth to one cub only every two to three years. Sometimes two cubs are born, but the second cub usually doesn't survive in the wild. In her lifetime, which can last about 20 years in the wild, a female giant panda may raise only five to eight cubs.

The Not-So-Giant Panda Baby

Panda cubs are tiny when they are born. They weigh three to five ounces (90 to 130 g) and can range in length from five to seven inches (12.7 to 17.8 cm). Scientists usually compare the size of a newborn giant panda to a stick of butter. Incredibly, a mama panda can be a thousand times heavier than her newborn cub! To put this into perspective, a human mother is about 20 times heavier than her newborn baby. Except for marsupials, such as koalas and kangaroos, the size difference between mother and baby panda is the biggest in the animal kingdom. This can be a problem, because a giant panda mother could accidentally roll over her cub.

A giant panda is born pink, with its eyes closed, a bit of fine hair sprinkled across its body, unable to crawl or walk, and completely helpless. Well, maybe not *completely* helpless.

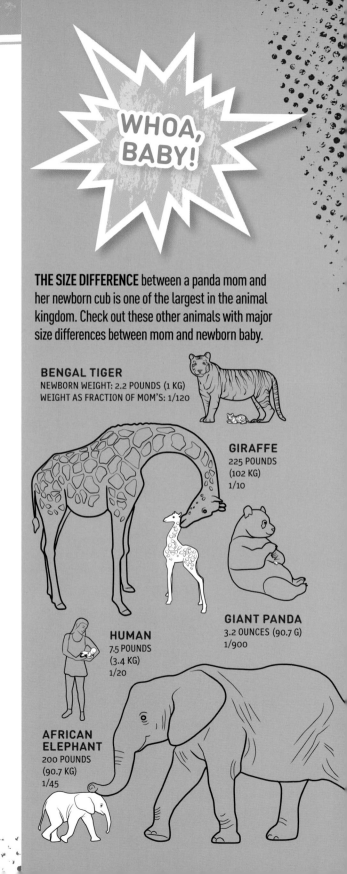

WHOA, BABY!

THE SIZE DIFFERENCE between a panda mom and her newborn cub is one of the largest in the animal kingdom. Check out these other animals with major size differences between mom and newborn baby.

BENGAL TIGER
NEWBORN WEIGHT: 2.2 POUNDS (1 KG)
WEIGHT AS FRACTION OF MOM'S: 1/120

GIRAFFE
225 POUNDS
(102 KG)
1/10

GIANT PANDA
3.2 OUNCES (90.7 G)
1/900

HUMAN
7.5 POUNDS
(3.4 KG)
1/20

AFRICAN ELEPHANT
200 POUNDS
(90.7 KG)
1/45

A NEWLY BORN PANDA CUB IS CARED FOR BY ANIMAL CARE STAFF.

A FOUR-WEEK-OLD PANDA CUB RESTS IN ITS MOTHER'S ARMS.

THESE PANDA CUBS REST AFTER ENJOYING PLAYTIME.

Giant panda cubs cry a lot, and their cries are loud. Crying helps the cub and mother get to know each other and bond. Crying also lets the mother know that the cub needs something, usually milk. A newborn cub spends all its time nursing and sleeping.

A panda cub needs a lot of attention during the first two months of its life. The mother panda needs to hold her cub close to keep it warm because a newborn cub can't regulate its body temperature. Mother pandas cradle their babies in their arms so their little ones can nurse, or drink their mothers' milk. Panda mothers are so devoted to their cub that they don't leave their den—they don't eat or drink—until their cub is a few days old.

One week after a cub is born, black patches start to appear on the cub's skin. The following week, black fur will start to grow in these areas. White fur will cover the panda's pink skin. After about four weeks, panda cubs start to open their eyes a bit. They're still blind, but their sense of smell is excellent. By the time they're eight weeks old, their eyes are fully open. And at about 11 weeks, cubs start to walk. Their eyesight and hearing get better, and their teeth start emerging.

By the time it's three and a half months old, a panda cub weighs more than 11 pounds (5 kg), and at four months the cub can stand and run and play, but it's still clumsy. By five months, a panda cub follows its mom around and starts to climb trees. They might sit in trees for hours, even days at a time. Up high in a tree, a panda cub is safe from predators.

Adult giant pandas don't have many predators, but their cubs do. Leopards are a cub's biggest threat. Jackals and yellow-throated martens also hunt giant panda cubs. But if any of these animals attack a panda cub, the mother panda will go into action. Giant pandas are skilled fighters when they have to be. Their large teeth and strong jaws really give pandas an edge with their natural predators. These choppers can deliver a nasty bite.

At six months old, a panda cub has all its baby teeth, its eyesight and hearing have improved, and it has started to eat—but it still nurses. At this age, panda cubs are at their roly-poliest. They're round and fluffy and clumsy and adorable.

By the time it's one year old, a panda cub weighs about 60 pounds (27 kg) and has its adult teeth. Most young giant pandas have completely stopped nursing by the time they're one and a half years old, which is when they're almost ready to go off on their own. Most giant pandas leave their moms by the time they're two years old. But it isn't until they're two and a half years old that giant pandas are nearly at their full adult height and weight. This is also the age when pandas start acting like adults, looking for territory and acting aggressively with other pandas.

This step away from their mother is a critical time for young pandas. Their survival depends on the life skills, such as searching for bamboo, claiming and protecting territory, and communicating, that they learned from their mother during their first two years of life.

A MOTHER PANDA PAYS CLOSE ATTENTION TO HER YOUNG CUB.

A TWO-AND-A-HALF-WEEK-OLD PANDA CUB

PANDA CUB TIMELINE

1 WEEK OLD

8 WEEKS

1 WEEK OLD
Black patches on the skin appear. Later, black fur will grow from those patches.

8 WEEKS
Cub's eyes are completely open. Cub's sense of smell is excellent. Cub stops crying.

MONTH 1   MONTH 2   MONTH 3   MONTH 4

5 WEEKS
Cub looks like a tiny adult.

16–21 WEEKS
Cub is running and playing.

4 WEEKS
Cub can regulate its temperature better, and its eyes begin to open. Mom leaves to eat bamboo. Cub's sense of smell develops. Cub weighs 4.4 pounds (2 kg). Cub doesn't cry as much.

16–21 WEEKS

4 WEEKS

11 WEEKS
Cub can stand and walk a bit. Cub starts teething, and cub's eyesight and hearing improve.

5 MONTHS
Cub follows mom and pretends to eat bamboo. Cub climbs and sits in trees.

10 MONTHS

5 MONTHS

10 MONTHS
Cub starts eating bamboo.

MONTH 6 | 7 | 8 | 9 | 10 | 11 | 12 | 13 | 14 | 15 | 16 | 17 | 18

6 MONTHS
Cub has baby teeth and tries to eat bamboo.

6 MONTHS

1½ TO 2 YEARS
Cub is weaned, which means it no longer drinks its mother's milk, and leaves mom.

1 YEAR

1 YEAR
Cub weighs up to 60 pounds (27 kg).

PANDA-MAZING!

GIANT PANDA ORIGAMI

Origami is the art of folding paper into three-dimensional (3D) objects. It was made popular by the Japanese, but many believe that since paper was invented in China, origami was likely to have been invented in China, too. Here's a fun and easy way to make an origami panda.

What you need:

1 SQUARE SHEET OF BLACK SINGLE-SIDED ORIGAMI PAPER (THE OTHER SIDE SHOULD BE WHITE)—YOU CAN FIND ORIGAMI PAPER AT MOST CRAFT STORES.

PROUDLY DISPLAY YOUR PANDA ORIGAMI!

BLACK MARKER

Step 1: With the white side up, fold the paper in half so it looks like a triangle and then in half again, and then open so the paper is flat.

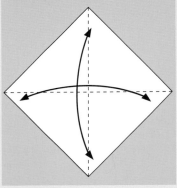

Step 2: Turn the paper at an angle so it looks like a diamond. Fold the right and left corners inward so each point is halfway to the center. The black side of the two corners should be visible.

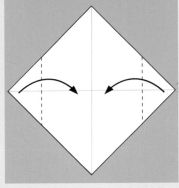

Step 3: With the black side of the two corners facing you, fold the paper back and in half, matching up the top and bottom corners.

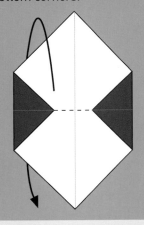

Step 4: Turn the paper so the black ears are on top.

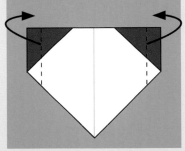

Step 5: Fold the bottom corner up about one-fourth of the way to the top.

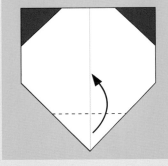

Step 6: Separate the two layers of paper on the bottom so you have a black diamond.

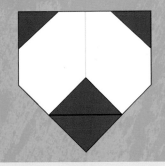

Step 7: Fold the bottom corner of the diamond up so its point meets the fold of the top layer.

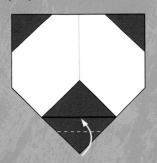

Step 8: Fold the bottom layer up at the fold line.

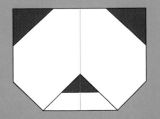

Step 9: Use the marker to draw the panda's eyes.

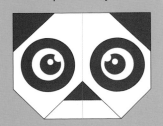

A GIANT PANDA PERCHES
ATOP A TREE IN A
MOUNTAINOUS AREA OF
SICHUAN PROVINCE, CHINA.

CHAPTER 3

AT HOME IN THE MOUNTAINS

INTRODUCTION

PANDA HABITAT IS A SENSORY EXPERIENCE OF SIGHTS , SOUNDS, AND SMELLS.

Few forests on Earth have the biodiversity that is found in the remote mountainous regions of central China. Only some tropical forests have a greater variety.

MARC BRODY

On a sunny and hot May afternoon, I drove up a road in a place called Happiness Valley (Xingfugou) at a far corner of the Wolong Nature Reserve in central China. Ironically, this "happiness" valley is a piece of land that was once a forest of trees and bamboo rich with wildlife, but it had been degraded by a long history of logging, farming, and livestock grazing. At the end of the road, I got out of the car and hiked up to a ridge, where I reached the entry gate to the Tiantai Shan giant panda reintroduction area. I unlocked the gate and stepped into the magical world of the giant panda.

The moment I walked through the gate, I left behind the heat of the worn-out land and entered the cool, refreshing air of a valley shaded by trees. Within 100 feet (30 m) of the gate, bamboo swayed in the mountain breeze. Along the path, the large buds of rhododendron trees were starting to bloom. As I got farther

down the path, tall birch trees encircled me, and a magical dappling of light danced through the leaves. Surrounding me was a vibrant forest, undisturbed by human activity, filled with a variety of wildlife. As I hiked up the mountain, I was thankful to be back in a place that felt like home.

Panda habitat is a great sensory experience of sounds, sights, and smells in one of the world's most diverse, plant-rich temperate forests—these are forests that have four seasons, including winter. Only some tropical forests, such as the Amazon rainforest, have a greater variety of plants than panda habitat.

I am fascinated by the diversity of plants and animals in this part of the world and by how every living thing in the forest is connected and relies on one another. A famous American conservationist named John Muir said, "When we try to pick out anything by itself, we find it hitched to everything else in the Universe." This quote and Muir's writing taught me that everything in nature is connected, and we should acknowledge all these connections and appreciate them.

When we carefully observe how plants and animals in the panda's diverse forests rely on one another, we gain a deeper understanding and respect for nature and what is required to sustain habitats for endangered species.

PANDA HABITATS LIKE TIANTAI SHAN HAVE SOME OF THE GREATEST DIVERSITY OF PLANTS AND ANIMALS OF ANYWHERE ON EARTH!

TIANTAI SHAN IS A GIANT PANDA REINTRODUCTION AREA. THIS IS WHERE PANDAS BORN IN CAPTIVITY WILL BE TRAINED BY THEIR MOTHERS AND REINTRODUCED INTO THE WILD.

MARC VISITS THE TIANTAI SHAN GIANT PANDA REINTRODUCTION AREA.

THE GIANT PANDA HAS BECOME A WORLDWIDE SYMBOL FOR ENVIRONMENTAL CAUSES AND FOR THE PEOPLE OF CHINA.

This charming black-and-white pudgy bear reminds people around the world of conservation, of saving Earth's plants and animals.

SHOWN IN ORANGE, THESE MOUNTAINOUS REGIONS OF CHINA—SICHUAN, SHAANXI, AND GANSU—ARE HOME TO CHINA'S WILD GIANT PANDAS.

SHAANXI

GANSU

C H I N A

SICHUAN

MOUNTAIN RANGES
- Min
- Qinling

INDIAN OCEAN

The Kingdom of Bamboo

In addition to reminding us of the importance of conservation, it's impossible to think about giant pandas without thinking about bamboo. After all, bamboo makes up 99 percent of a panda's diet, and China is home to about 15 million acres (6 million ha) of bamboo forests, making it the country with the most bamboo. It's no wonder that China is called the Kingdom of Bamboo.

Most giant pandas live in patches of forest along six different mountain ranges. The mountains are in the Chinese provinces of Sichuan, Shaanxi, and Gansu. Provinces are parts of a country

ONE OF THE PANDAS THAT LIVE IN THE WOLONG NATURE RESERVE

that have their own government. They are somewhat like states. The Sichuan Province is home to nearly 80 percent of the wild giant pandas. It is so famous for pandas that it's nicknamed the Home of the Giant Panda.

Within the Gansu, Sichuan, and Shaanxi Provinces, pandas live in around 20 isolated habitats. The Min and Qinling Mountains are where most wild giant pandas live. The Min Mountains, also called the Minshan Mountains, are a mountain range that spreads across the Sichuan and Gansu Provinces in central China. These mountains have peaks reaching more than 18,000 feet (5,490 m).

THESE MASSIVE MOUNTAINS TOP OFF AT 12,359 FEET (3,767.02 M).

PACIFIC OCEAN

TAIWAN

MOUNT HUA, IN THE QINLING MOUNTAINS IN SHAANXI PROVINCE, SHOWN HERE, IS ONE OF THE FIVE GREAT MOUNTAINS OF CHINA.

But giant pandas don't normally wander above 11,000 feet (3,355 m), probably because trees don't grow above that height. About 300 giant pandas live in the steep, thick forests of the Min Mountains.

A smaller number of wild giant pandas also live in the Qinling Mountains in the Shaanxi Province. These huge mountains, with the highest peak topping off at 12,359 feet (3,767.02 m), form a natural west-east barrier between northern and southern China and are home to about 200 to 300 giant pandas. The Qinling Mountains are also home to the rarely seen brown-and-white Qinling panda.

TALL STALKS IN A BAMBOO FOREST IN CHENGDU, SICHUAN PROVINCE, CHINA.

Under the Canopy

The giant panda lives in some of China's cool, humid bamboo forests between 5,000 and 10,000 feet (1,525 and 3,050 m) high in the mountains. Most of the bamboo forests that make up the giant panda's habitat have old-growth conifers and deciduous broad-leaved trees that tower over the bamboo. Trees that have needles and cones, like pine trees, are conifers. Most conifers are evergreen trees, meaning their leaves remain green all year round and don't drop in the fall. Trees that lose their leaves in the fall, like birch trees, are deciduous.

Old-growth forests are special because

LAYERS OF THE FOREST

EMERGENT LAYER

This is the **TALLEST LAYER** of the forest and has the most exposure to elements like sun, rain, and wind. The animals that live in the emergent layer are birds, monkeys, rodents, snakes, and insects.

CANOPY

This layer gets some sunlight and rain. The leaves and branches of the trees in this layer spread out **LIKE A ROOF** over the layers below. Deciduous broad-leaved trees often make up the forest canopy. Animals that live in the emergent layer also live in the forest canopy.

UNDERSTORY

Shade-loving plants, including bamboo, thrive in this layer of the forest where they are **PROTECTED FROM HARSH WIND AND SUNLIGHT.** This layer is damp and warmer than the layers above. Large animals like leopards share the understory with smaller animals like red pandas and squirrels.

FOREST FLOOR

This is the **DARKEST AND DAMPEST LAYER.** Not much sunlight gets to the forest floor. This layer is teeming with insects and other animals that thrive on the emerging and decomposing vegetation. Here you'll find many animals like giant pandas, pheasants, and the goat-like takin.

OLD-GROWTH FORESTS ARE MADE UP OF PLANTS AND TREES THAT HAVE BEEN GROWING FOR 150 YEARS OR MORE.

BAMBOO FORMS THE UNDERSTORY IN AN OLD-GROWTH FOREST IN CHINA.

they're naturally occurring forests with a variety of plants and animals, and they have been growing for at least 150 years without any major disturbances from human activity. Because of its age, an old-growth forest has many layers. Some of the main layers include the forest floor, understory, canopy, and emergent layer. The forest floor, or lowest layer, is littered with dead leaves and a fallen dead tree here and there. Not much sunlight gets to the forest floor, so throughout most of the forest, only low-growing plants, such as ferns, can grow there. The understory is the next layer. It gets more light than the forest floor, but it's protected by the canopy above it from elements such as wind and bright sunlight. In old-growth forests that contain bamboo, the bamboo is part of the understory layer. Growing above the understory is the canopy. In a panda's habitat, deciduous broad-leaved trees often make up the forest canopy. The emergent layer is the very top of the

tallest trees. Conifers tend to be the emergent layer in bamboo forests.

These old-growth forests create a unique and varied environment, and they are the only place giant pandas can live in the wild. It makes sense, then, that the biggest threat to giant pandas, and the biggest reason the giant panda population is so low, is habitat loss. So how did giant pandas lose so much of their habitat, and what can be done to bring at least some of it back?

A Shrinking Home

Thousands of years ago, more than 100,000 giant pandas may have roamed the lowlands and mountains from southern China to the northern areas around Beijing. They even lived south of China into Southeast Asia. But over the last four hundred years, the human population in China has grown. People started moving farther into wild areas, including bamboo forests. Slowly the

OLD-GROWTH FORESTS ARE SOMETIMES CLEARED TO MAKE WAY FOR FARMLAND, LIKE THIS AREA IN SICHUAN PROVINCE, CHINA.

STEEL MILLS BUILT ALONG A RIVER IN CHINA

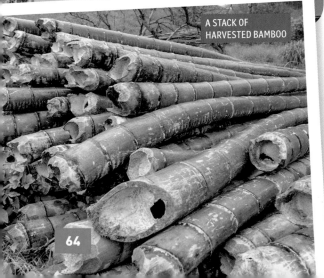
A STACK OF HARVESTED BAMBOO

bamboo forests (and other forested areas) were cut down and turned into farmland. A great amount of the giant panda's habitat was destroyed, and the pandas were forced to retreat high into the mountains.

Beginning in the late 1700s, in other parts of the world, new industries drove the building of factories, motorized vehicles, and machinery, and the products generated by these industries were being introduced into everyday life. People were excited about the new inventions that were being manufactured. That enthusiasm drove demand and kept production going.

At about that same time, beginning in the mid-1700s, the Chinese population began to grow quickly. All these people needed to be fed, and new types of seeds and farming methods helped agriculture grow in the country. It wasn't until the late 1980s that industry and manufacturing burst into the lives of many of the Chinese people. China quickly changed from a fairly poor agricultural country into a cutting-edge producer of steel, ships, robots, cars, computers, cell phones, and much, much more. This increase in production meant more buildings and more roads. Cities grew, pushing development even farther into rural areas and wildlands.

By 2010, China led the world in industrial manufacturing. But these industries didn't replace agriculture. Farming was thriving. It just had been pushed farther out into the wilderness. To accommodate this new way of life, logging and the clearing of land increased, and roads, houses, schools, and office buildings all invaded the rural and wild areas.

Development happened so quickly, in a matter of decades, that people didn't stop to think about the effects on the environment. As it was with all industrial countries, by the time most people realized their activities could harm

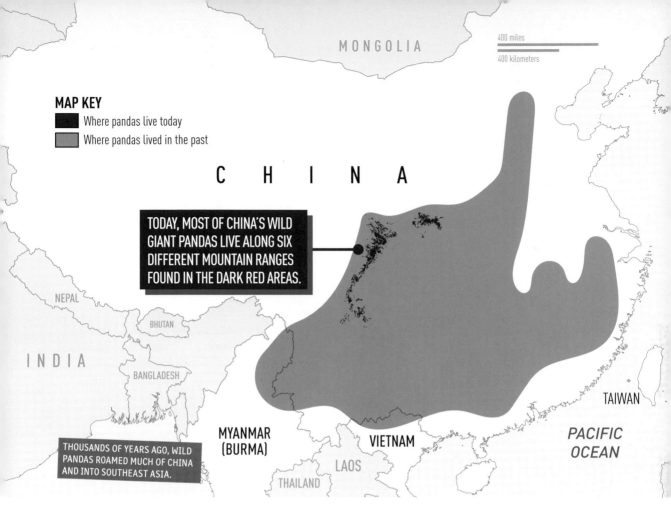

MONGOLIA

400 miles

400 kilometers

MAP KEY
- Where pandas live today
- Where pandas lived in the past

C H I N A

TODAY, MOST OF CHINA'S WILD GIANT PANDAS LIVE ALONG SIX DIFFERENT MOUNTAIN RANGES FOUND IN THE DARK RED AREAS.

NEPAL

BHUTAN

INDIA

BANGLADESH

THOUSANDS OF YEARS AGO, WILD PANDAS ROAMED MUCH OF CHINA AND INTO SOUTHEAST ASIA.

MYANMAR (BURMA)

VIETNAM

LAOS

THAILAND

TAIWAN

PACIFIC OCEAN

the habitat and lives of plants and animals, a lot of damage had already been done. And in China, some of that damage had a major impact on giant pandas and bamboo forests.

Giant pandas had already been pushed out of their lowland habitat to live mainly in the mountains. Living in the mountains is nothing new to giant pandas. But they used to be able to spread out into the lowland forests, which are below 3,281 feet (1,000 m). And pandas that did live in the mountains would migrate down to the lowlands during winter and spring to eat the bamboo that was growing in the milder climate.

As giant panda habitat becomes smaller, pandas will be forced to live in tighter quarters, in territories smaller than the average

2.3 square miles (6 sq km) that a panda prefers. Fewer resources, such as bamboo and dens, will be available to support a panda's daily needs to stay alive. This will cause more fighting among pandas over land and food. Smaller territories and lack of food and places to raise cubs will also lead to a drop in reproduction, which means fewer pandas.

Decreasing the giant panda's habitat is not the only effect of human activity. Barriers such as farmland, roads, quarries, dams, and train tracks have fragmented, or broken up, the giant panda's range into a mosaic of unconnected land, which nearly drove the giant panda to extinction. When giant pandas can't cross these barriers, they can't get to part of their territory. This may keep a panda from

NOT SO COOL
FOR BAMBOO

THE BAMBOO THAT GROWS in giant panda habitats thrives in the cool, misty climate of mountain forests. But climate change is beginning to affect bamboo. Climate is what we call the average weather of an area over a number of years. For instance, the United States has areas with varying climates. Southern states tend to have a warm climate and don't often experience freezing temperatures, whereas northern states tend to have a cold climate with winters of snow and ice. Climate change is a change in weather patterns over a long period of time. We're talking thousands or even millions of years, not just a few months.

But recently, scientific studies have shown that climate change, specifically the warming of our planet, due in large part to the increasing effects of greenhouse gases, is happening at a much faster pace than in the past. This rate of warming is causing problems for many plants and animals, including, of course, pandas and their main food—bamboo. If global warming continues, China's bamboo forests will likely die.

GREENHOUSE EFFECT: SOME SOLAR RADIATION IS REFLECTED BACK OUT TO SPACE. BUT SOME SOLAR RADIATION IS TRAPPED BY GASES LIKE CARBON DIOXIDE AND METHANE.

SOLAR RADIATION ABSORBED AND TRAPPED by carbon dioxide, methane, and other gases

SOLAR RADIATION

REFLECTION OF SOLAR RADIATION out to space

finding a mate or cut the panda off from food supplies or water. If pandas can't find mates, they can't have cubs, which means they can't help their population grow. If they don't have food or a source of drinking water, like a lake or a stream, nearby, they will die.

Some of the roads were built for logging, which wiped out large swaths of forest, leaving the land bare. The trees were cut down so they could be made into items such as furniture, paper, and toys. Bamboo was also logged. Even though it's a grass, bamboo has a woody stem that can be made into useful products such as flooring, chopsticks, and even bed sheets. Logging did its damage, but it is not as much of a factor today since the Chinese government banned logging in 17 provinces in 1998. Unfortunately, illegal logging still occurs, and new roads and train tracks continue to crisscross the land.

Mother Nature has also contributed to the giant panda's habitat loss. Although pandas have survived thousands of years of natural disasters, habitat loss and fragmentation caused by human activity have made recovering from natural disasters difficult, if not impossible. Earthquakes and landslides destroy trees and bamboo and can wipe out parts of the panda's habitat. And three fairly recent earthquakes have shaken the giant panda's world: the Songpan earthquake in 1976, the Wenchuan earthquake (also known as the Sichuan earthquake) in 2008, and the Ya'an earthquake in 2013. Some scientists have estimated that 70 percent of the habitat loss between 2001 and 2003 was caused by the Wenchuan earthquake and the landslides that followed. Although scientists debate the exact amount of habitat loss this natural disaster caused, it was a setback for the giant panda and its habitat.

EARTHQUAKES AND LANDSLIDES DESTROY TREES AND BAMBOO AND CAN WIPE OUT PARTS OF THE PANDA'S HABITAT.

WORKERS FEED THE PANDAS AT THE WOLONG BREEDING CENTER, ONE DAY AFTER THE 7.9 MAGNITUDE WENCHUAN EARTHQUAKE.

A POWERFUL QUAKE

THE 2008 WENCHUAN EARTHQUAKE was so strong that it destroyed the homes of 4.3 million people, and 69,000 people lost their lives. It was just as devastating to the natural world. Scientists studied satellite photos comparing forests before and after the earthquake. They saw that more than 130 square miles (337 sq km) of panda habitat was destroyed, leaving nothing behind but bare land.

BUILDINGS CRUMBLED DUE TO THE FORCE OF THE WENCHUAN EARTHQUAKE.

BAMBOO CULMS ARE MOSTLY HOLLOW!

DRIED BAMBOO POLES ARE STACKED IN PILES.

BAMBOO CAN BE A STRONG BUILDING MATERIAL. HERE, IT BORDERS A GARDEN IN SUZHOU, JIANGSU PROVINCE, CHINA.

Solving the problem of how to expand and protect the giant panda's shrinking, fragmented habitat and help increase their population is not an easy task. No single solution or course of action exists. We know why and how giant pandas have found themselves sprinkled in small, isolated pockets of central China's mountains. But enlarging their habitat and increasing their numbers takes a lot of coordination among scientists, politicians, and the Chinese people. It's slow going.

Luckily, people can't help falling in love with these big, lumbering, comical bears, and most everyone wants to help these endangered animals. The key to the giant panda's well-being is ensuring they have habitat safe from human development and a healthy bamboo forest. The more we understand how bamboo thrives, the more successful our efforts will be in helping the giant panda.

The Giant of Grasses

Bamboo is the giant of grasses, with some types of bamboo growing higher than 130 feet (40 m) in only one growing season, which spans from spring to fall. Sometimes, bamboo will grow a couple of feet (meters) in just one day!

Bamboo has been around for nearly 40 million years as a source of food for plant-eating animals.

BAMBOO CAN BE FASHIONED INTO USEFUL HOUSEHOLD ITEMS LIKE BOWLS AND STEAMERS.

And for the last 7,000 years or so, people have carved bamboo into arrows, mashed it into paper, cut it into building materials, and more. Scientists believe that bamboo originated in China, but different types of bamboo grow everywhere in the world except where the climate is very cold.

Bamboo is an evergreen perennial. Perennials are plants such as day lilies and irises that live through two or more growing seasons. This grass is often mistakenly called a tree because of its height and strong woodlike stem, which is called a culm. The culm is different from tree trunks in many ways. A culm that's just breaking through the ground is already as thick as it's ever going to be. Compare that to trees, which are skinny little saplings when they're young and continue to expand as they grow. Once grown, a culm is flexible despite its toughness, whereas a tree trunk doesn't bend at all. Culms are mostly hollow, but trees are solid. A culm grows in sections called internodes, and each internode is separated by what looks like a raised ring that's called a node. Although the culms of most bamboo are hollow, the nodes are solid. Branches and leaves grow from the nodes. Like culms, bamboo branches are formed by nodes and internodes.

Dining on Bamboo

Of the more than 1,200 species of bamboo that grow in the world, giant pandas eat around 60. But all 60 types of bamboo don't grow together in one area. For giant pandas to thrive in the wild, at least two species of bamboo need to be growing in their territory. This isn't to keep pandas from getting bored with just one flavor of bamboo. It all has to do with nutrition and how bamboo grows.

Giant pandas are foragers and spend their days wandering around looking for bamboo to eat.

CULM

INTERNODE
(SECTION BETWEEN NODES)

NODE

STALKS OF BAMBOO SHOW THEIR CULMS, INTERNODES, AND NODES.

They eat the shoots, culms, and leaves of a bamboo, but they don't eat all these bamboo parts in one sitting. The amount and type of nutrition in shoots, culms, and leaves change depending on the season and the species of bamboo. Because of this, pandas tend to eat certain parts of bamboo during certain times of the year to get the variety of nutrients they need to stay healthy.

In the spring, young bamboo shoots start to grow. To a panda, shoots are the most delicious part of the bamboo. They're also the most nutritious part and easiest to digest. When summer comes along, new bamboo isn't growing anymore, and the shoots are becoming tall and woody. Bamboo is putting energy into growing its leaves, so the giant panda's meal changes from shoots to leaves. By fall, bamboo leaves have become less nutritious. As winter comes along, bamboo becomes dormant, or stops growing. This allows the bamboo to save its energy for the next growing season, when it is warmer and rainier. Winter is when the bamboo's stem, or culm, is the most nutritious.

Depending on the species, bamboo grows at different elevations, from lowlands to high in the mountains. Temperatures change at different elevations,

A PANDA NIBBLES BAMBOO LEAVES DURING SUMMERTIME.

THE CALCIUM IN BAMBOO IS PARTICULARLY NUTRITIOUS FOR GIANT PANDA MOMS THAT ARE NURSING THEIR BABIES.

ARROW BAMBOO IS ONE OF THE GIANT PANDA'S FAVORITE VARIETIES OF BAMBOO.

BAMBOO LEAVES HAVE A LOT OF CALCIUM.

which can cause similar plants to grow at different times of the year. Giant pandas often migrate, or move, up and down their mountain homes in search of bamboo that is growing the most nutritious parts at that time. Having two or more species of bamboo in an area ensures pandas are getting all the nutrients they need throughout the year. A good example of this can be found in the Qinling Mountains.

In the spring, giant pandas eat the shoots of the umbrella bamboo. This time of year is known as "shooting season." Bamboo shoots contain a lot of phosphorous and nitrogen. They have the right amount of nutrients that female pandas need when they are getting ready to mate. When the shoots become bigger and less nutritious, the pandas trek higher up the mountain, where the arrow bamboo are just starting their shooting season.

Once the shoots have grown to their full height, the bamboo's energy switches from growing shoots to growing leaves. The leaves then become the most nutritious part of the bamboo. By early July, the arrow bamboo leaves are growing. Bamboo leaves have a lot of calcium. This comes just in time for panda cubs to develop within their mothers, since calcium is needed for bone growth. When the arrow bamboo leaves stop growing, the pandas lumber back down the mountain to eat the leaves of the umbrella bamboo. As luck, or nature, would have it, these bamboo leaves are fully grown at about the time panda moms are nursing their cubs. The calcium-rich leaves help giant panda moms produce milk to feed their cubs after they're born.

The variety and life cycle of bamboo—as well as a large enough habitat to support these plants—are examples of why protecting the giant panda's habitat is just as important as protecting the giant panda.

THE WORLD'S SMALLEST BAMBOO

NOT ALL SPECIES OF BAMBOO ARE GIANT. Some are small, growing only a few inches high. A recently discovered species of bamboo (*Raddiella vanessiae*) doesn't even make it to an inch. It's the world's smallest bamboo. Found in French Guiana in South America, it grows to be only three-quarters of an inch (2 cm) tall.

IT'S SMALL ENOUGH TO FIT IN THE PALM OF A HAND!

TEENY TINY BAMBOO!

RADDIELLA VANESSIAE IS LESS THAN AN INCH TALL.

A SLICED CROSS SECTION OF BAMBOO

HOLLOW INTERNODES ARE SEPARATED BY THE NODES.

HERE'S THE BAMBOO'S RHIZOME, PART OF ITS ROOT STRUCTURE.

BAMBOO FLOWERS APPEAR ONLY ONCE IN A BAMBOO PLANT'S LIFE.

Killer Flowers

Believe it or not, many of the bamboo in a forest are clones. They are identical. Bamboo shoots sprout from the plant's horizontally growing stems, called rhizomes, which are part of its root system. As the rhizomes spread, so does the bamboo. In this way, a few individual bamboo can fill an entire forest. This feature, though, also makes bamboo open to mass die-offs. If a disease hits one bamboo, all its clones may be infected as well.

ARROW BAMBOO FLOWERS AFTER 60 YEARS.

Flowering bamboo can be deadly, too. A bamboo flowers just once in its life, and then it dies. Scientists think this happens so seedlings don't have to compete with the full-grown plants for sunlight, water, and nutrients from the soil. Once the roots have died along with the rhizomes, it may take up to two years for a bamboo plant to appear dead. That alone wouldn't be so bad. After all, the forest is filled with thousands of bamboo plants. The problem is that flowering happens en masse—to all the bamboo clones at the same time. Giant pandas won't eat bamboo once it has flowered, so this mass flowering can leave giant pandas with very little or nothing to eat.

WORLDWIDE FLOWERING

THE LONGEST TIME BETWEEN A BAMBOO'S MASS FLOWERING WAS 130 YEARS.

Phyllostachys bambusoides, a giant timber bamboo, originated in China but can now be found in many countries around the world. About every 120 years when it's time to flower, all *Phyllostachys bambusoides* plants around the world burst into bloom at the same time. Then they all die. Because of careful record keeping, we know this species flowered in the years 999 and 1114. It also flowered sometime in the early 1700s, between 1844 and 1847, and in the late 1960s. You'll have to wait until around 2090 to see the giant timber bamboo's next mass flowering.

A GROVE OF *PHYLLOSTACHYS BAMBUSOIDES* IN FRANCE

The past few mass flowerings were deadly for many giant pandas. In the 1970s, more than 138 pandas died of starvation because of the flowering and dying bamboo. Between 1983 and 1986, another mass flowering of bamboo resulted in the starvation deaths of at least 62 wild pandas.

Thankfully, bamboo flowering doesn't happen often. Some bamboo are more than a hundred years old before they flower. Arrow bamboo, one of the species that giant pandas eat, takes more than 10 years for the bamboo to mature, then flowers at 60 years.

A FEMALE GIANT PANDA GNAWS ON A BAMBOO SHOOT.

This bamboo die-off isn't as much of a problem if two or more bamboo species grow in the same area—as long as they aren't on the same flowering schedule. And it wasn't a problem years ago before the giant panda's habitat was fragmented. At that time, all a panda had to do was migrate to another area where bamboo wasn't flowering. Today, the Chinese government is working to connect the panda's fragmented habitat as one way to help giant pandas. Let's take a look at other ways China is helping pandas.

GIANT PANDAS LOUNGE AROUND AT THE CHENGDU RESEARCH BASE OF GIANT PANDA BREEDING.

IT'S A BEAR HUG!

A PANDA PLAYS WITH A STAFF MEMBER AT THE WOLONG BREEDING CENTER.

China to the Rescue!

One way people protect animals is through their government because governments have the power to pass laws that protect animals and their habitats. In China, laws have been passed that make it illegal for people to hunt giant pandas or cut down trees in panda habitat. China has also set aside most of the giant panda's habitat as nature reserves and protected areas. The country has also built research centers and breeding facilities for scientists to use to study giant panda biology and behavior, to learn how to help increase the giant panda's population.

Most of the giant panda reserves and research centers have been set up for at least some of the following purposes:

- Protect the forest, habitat, or bamboo
- Monitor the areas for illegal hunting or logging
- Provide corridors, or pathways, from one fragmented habitat to another
- Search for sick or injured pandas and get them to a panda hospital if needed
- Assist with research and conduct studies of giant pandas
- Educate visitors and local residents about giant pandas and the benefits of protecting them
- Support people living nearby so they'll respect the protected area

In the 1940s, the Chinese government decided to stop people from coming to China to capture and take pandas to other countries. During this period, China also began conservation efforts to repair the giant panda's habitat. This, of course, helped the giant panda as well as all other wildlife living within that habitat. By the early 1960s, hunting and catching giant pandas without the government's permission were forbidden, and China had four nature reserves set aside especially for giant pandas. These reserves were areas in the wild where pandas could live freely.

Today, 3,459,400 acres (1,400,000 ha) of forestland in China have been set aside in 67 reserves for giant pandas. This covers about half the giant panda's habitat and is home to almost 70 percent of China's wild giant pandas. Along with these reserves, corridors—or pathways—have been developed between fragmented bits of habitat. Through these corridors, giant pandas can move to other areas for food and to find potential mates.

In 2017, China made a big announcement. It revealed a plan to link together much of the fragmented giant panda habitat—including the 67 already established reserves—into one giant park. This park will span the three provinces that giant pandas call home—Gansu, Shaanxi, and Sichuan Provinces. It will be almost 10,500 square miles (27,200 sq km), which is about three times the size of Yellowstone National Park in the United States. The Chinese park will include 80 percent of the panda groups and 70 percent of their habitat. Where will the Chinese government find an area that large that is unpopulated? They can't. To make this reserve, China will be moving more than 170,000 people who currently live on that land to new locations.

A SCULPTURE OUTSIDE THE CHENGDU RESEARCH BASE OF GIANT PANDA BREEDING

HELP IS ON THE WAY, OR IS IT?

TOWARD THE END OF THE 1980s, about 1,100 giant pandas were thought to be living in China's bamboo forests. This shockingly low number was a call to action for many organizations. Programs to raise money, pass laws, and make positive changes to help giant pandas and their habitat ramped up. One such program was called Grain for Green, and it has become the biggest forest tree-planting project in the world. But has it been successful?

The goal of the Grain for Green program is to stop flooding and land erosion caused by tearing down forests to make way for farmland. With no trees to hold the soil in place or absorb water, rains carry the soil and other sediment away, causing erosion. Heavy rains that cannot be absorbed by the soil or trees result in flooding. The program offers farmers food or money to plant trees on their farmland to return the land to forests. The Grain for Green program has raised enough funds over the years to pay farmers to plant trees in an area about the size of New Mexico.

HEAVY FLOODING, LIKE THIS IN JIANG'AN IN SICHUAN PROVINCE, CAN BE CAUSED BY TEARING DOWN FORESTS.

This tree-planting effort helped many farmers out of poverty, and it did stop the flooding, but it didn't do much to help the giant panda and other wildlife of the region. Why? The problem is that in most areas, only one type of tree was planted, and it wasn't the type of tree naturally found in giant panda habitat.

A variety of plants and animals are necessary for a healthy habitat. Only planting trees, especially just one species of tree, isn't enough to reestablish a habitat. This new "forest" supported less plant and animal life than the farmland had. Worst of all, it wasn't suitable as a giant panda habitat because no one had planted bamboo in these new forests.

In addition to the giant pandas, thousands of other animals and plants will benefit from the establishment of the new Chinese park. All wildlife in the area will have a healthier and safer environment to live in, away from human intrusion.

The Chinese people who have to move from their homes to make way for the reserve have been offered new places to live, and some have the option of working on the reserve. Those who decide to work in the park will be trained to help with different aspects of running the park, including acting as guides for tourists. That's right. While protecting giant pandas and their habitat, the government will welcome tourists to enjoy the protected areas and learn about the important work of protecting the environment for all living creatures.

Stores and restaurants and transportation to and from the park will all be available to visitors. With the popularity of the reserves that are already in existence in China, this grand park is sure to be enjoyed by many people.

Some worry, though, that too much emphasis will be put on tourism instead of focusing on re-creating a continuous giant panda habitat and increasing the panda population. That's one reason it's important for all of us to continue helping giant pandas.

SAY CHEESE! THIS PANDA'S PHOTO WAS TAKEN WITH A MOTION-DETECTING CAMERA, WHICH SNAPS A PIC WHEN ITS SENSORS PICK UP MOVEMENT.

CAUGHT ON PANDA CAM! A GIANT PANDA ON A SNOWY DAY IN THE BAISHUIJIANG NATIONAL NATURE RESERVE, GANSU PROVINCE, CHINA.

OBSERVING PANDAS IN THE WILD

GIANT PANDAS ARE FAMOUS FOR A LOT OF REASONS. For the scientists who want to study pandas in the wild, giant pandas are most famous for being shy and hard to find. Many scientists who have been studying wild pandas for years have never actually seen one. But now they have a tool for keeping tabs on the elusive bears.

Scientists set up motion-detecting cameras in a part of the forest where they think giant pandas might wander through. Then they leave and wait. The cameras run day and night. Any time a camera detects motion, it snaps a picture. Scientists call this a camera trap.

The information scientists get from these cameras is not just about giant pandas. Other animals also set off the cameras, so scientists can see and learn more about other animals that share the panda's habitat. Two such animals are the leopard cat and the red panda.

A MOTION-DETECTING CAMERA

THREATENED ANIMALS AROUND THE WORLD

THE FUZZY AND ADORABLE GIANT PANDA has inspired people and governments across the globe to invest serious time and money to save it from extinction—more than has any other species! But there are lots of other amazing animals around the world that are threatened. Here are just a few, with their IUCN Red List status. To learn more about these animals, or other animals that live in your area, get an adult's permission to go online to *worldwildlife.org/species*.

ARCTIC

ASIA

PACIFIC OCEAN

NORTH AMERICA

ASIA

CALIFORNIA CONDOR:
CRITICALLY ENDANGERED

THE CALIFORNIA CONDOR IS THREATENED BY HABITAT LOSS, INJURY FROM FLYING INTO POWER LINES, AND POISONING FROM INGESTING HUNTERS' BULLETS LEFT IN ANIMAL CARCASSES.

JAVAN RHINO:
CRITICALLY ENDANGERED

New Zealand

KAKAPO:
CRITICALLY ENDANGERED

THE KAKAPO IS THREATENED BY HABITAT LOSS AND THE INTRODUCTION OF RAT AND CAT PREDATORS.

THE JAVAN RHINO IS THREATENED BY HABITAT LOSS AND HUNTING.

OCEAN

THE MEDITERRANEAN MONK SEAL IS THREATENED BY HABITAT DESTRUCTION AND BY INJURY FROM BEING TRAPPED IN FISHING NETS.

BROWN SPIDER MONKEY:
CRITICALLY ENDANGERED

EUROPE

THE BROWN SPIDER MONKEY IS THREATENED BY HUNTING AND HABITAT LOSS.

MEDITERRANEAN MONK SEAL:
ENDANGERED

AFRICA

INDIAN OCEAN

SOUTH AMERICA

THE AFRICAN ELEPHANT IS THREATENED BY HABITAT LOSS AND HUNTING.

ATLANTIC OCEAN

AFRICAN ELEPHANT:
VULNERABLE

ANTARCTICA

79

PANDA-MAZING!

CREATE YOUR OWN WILDLIFE HABITAT

Although you can't create a habitat for giant pandas in your backyard (since it's unlikely you have pandas wandering in your neighborhood), you can still create a habitat for wildlife. Invite birds, small animals, and insects into your yard by planting native flowers and seed-producing plants, building bird houses, or adding bird feeders. Once you have your habitat set up, you can observe all the goings-on in your yard.

What you need:

BIRDBATH

GARDEN GLOVES AND TROWEL

SEEDS OR SEEDLINGS OF NATIVE PLANTS

WATERING CAN

Instructions:

Step 1: Ask your parents if you can have a small part of the backyard to create your habitat. Pull weeds, dig up plants, and remove any other debris so just the soil remains.

Step 2: Research the types of plants that are native to your area, especially ones that birds, butterflies, and bees love. You can go to a local zoo or arboretum, you can look on the internet with an adult to get ideas, or your local nursery can direct you to the native plants that it sells. It's best to get native plants while they're still small.

TIP:
Plants reproduce, and people often dig out plants' sprouts and seedlings and throw them away. Ask your neighbors if they have any native plants they want to get rid of. You can also buy seed mixes of native plants. Follow the package directions and watch your plants sprout. Be sure to keep the soil moist for the first couple of weeks. Some plants you might want to consider are those that are food sources for different types of animals. These could be sunflowers, milkweed, and safflower.

Step 3: Once you have your plants or seeds gathered, plant them in the ground and use your watering can to give them a good soaking.

Step 4: Add a birdbath and fill it with water, and watch birds and other animals stop by for a dip or a drink. Be sure to replace the water daily.

TIP:
Don't use pesticides to control weeds. Instead, pull them yourself.

Step 5: Get up close to your plants and see if you can find insect eggs or caterpillars on the leaves. Depending on where you live and what you've planted, keep an eye out for ants and anthills, praying mantises and grasshoppers, butterflies and moths, and lizards and geckos. Remember to only look at—don't touch—any animal visitor.

Step 6: Make sure to water your plants regularly. Then sit back and watch as the creatures in your area come to enjoy your habitat!

TWO-YEAR-OLD PANDA ZHANG XIANG, BORN IN CAPTIVITY, TAKES HER FIRST STEPS IN NATURE AS SHE'S RELEASED INTO THE WILD.

大熊猫 "张想" 放归

中国保护大熊猫研究中心

CHAPTER 4

OUT OF THE WILD—AND BACK AGAIN!

INTRODUCTION

ONE AFTERNOON I WAS DRIVING FROM MY HOME IN THE COUNTRYSIDE

into the city, and my nature-loving five-year-old daughter noticed more and more houses and roads were being built all around us.

MARC BRODY

I'll always remember what she said: "I love nature, and it keeps going away."

She was right. Throughout our world, natural land has been fragmented and replaced by human settlements, roads, neighborhoods, and shopping and industrial areas. More and more of the natural world is disappearing.

In response, conservationists, like me, work hard to protect nature and wildlife. The biggest challenge is saving and restoring enough habitat for giant pandas and endangered species to survive in the wild.

The problem of lost habitat isn't unique to giant pandas. Gorillas, rhinos, and leopards are just a few of the other animals that are being squeezed out of their homes. But thankfully, there is growing hope for giant pandas. Scientists and veterinarians have made outstanding progress in breeding and caring for hundreds of captive giant pandas in zoos and captive breeding centers. Now captive-born pandas are being trained to be reintroduced into the wild.

For wild panda populations to survive in the future, we need to reverse habitat fragmentation and restore wildlife corridors. Wildlife corridors will be lifelines for pandas, allowing them to move across the landscape to find healthy bamboo, establish their own home territories, and mate.

Our efforts to save habitat will be complicated by our warming climate. We will have to restore the corridors with native plant species that will tolerate warmer weather. Such restoration can help other endangered species as well.

While these are big challenges, don't feel powerless. The good news is that no matter where we live, each of us can make a difference by caring for and improving the environment. You can start by visiting a nearby park or nursery and asking if there is a restoration project in your area. You can also ask your teachers or parents to help you and your friends find places where you can help restore habitat.

The key to habitat restoration starts with you making a commitment to be kind to and care for our natural world. You can help the environment—and help giant pandas and other endangered animals live in the wild for generations to come.

LIVESTOCK USED TO GRAZE IN THIS PASTURE IN THE WOLONG NATURE RESERVE. CHINA IS WORKING TO ENFORCE LAWS TO PROTECT LAND IN NATURE RESERVES FROM FURTHER DAMAGE.

TRAIL LEADING TO TIANTAI SHAN GIANT PANDA REINTRODUCTION AREA

HELPING TO PRESERVE AND RESTORE HABITAT SO ANIMALS CAN LIVE AND THRIVE IN THE WILD IS A KEY PART OF PROTECTING PANDAS—AND ANY THREATENED SPECIES.

MARC WORKS WITH STUDENTS TO PLAN FIELD ACTIVITIES FOCUSED ON RESTORING HABITAT.

IN THE EARLY 1900S NO ONE IN THE UNITED STATES HAD EVER SEEN A LIVE PANDA.

That all changed in 1936, when America met a giant panda named Su Lin. He became an instant celebrity.

From Exotic Spectacle to National Treasure

In 1869, a French priest and zoologist returned from China, bringing with him a giant panda pelt. This was the first time westerners had heard about the giant panda's existence. Why? During the late 19th century, travel to other continents was a long and expensive journey that was taken by ship. People didn't have much of an opportunity to see animals from other countries. But a few natural history museums did feature taxidermic animals from all over the world. Taxidermy is when a dead animal is preserved and mounted in a lifelike stance. People would visit these natural history museums to see spectacular creatures they had only read or heard about.

In 1936, the first living giant panda was brought to the United States by Ruth Harkness. She was a fashion designer whose husband had died while trekking the mountains of China in search of giant pandas. She decided to continue his search to bring a live giant panda back home. She found an orphaned cub she named Su Lin, and she brought him back with her. Su Lin was not only the first living panda brought to the United States, he was also the first living panda to leave China. Su Lin lived with Harkness for several months until she sold him to Chicago's Brookfield Zoo. Not surprisingly, he became an instant celebrity.

A POSTER ANNOUNCING SU LIN'S ARRIVAL AT THE BROOKFIELD ZOO

THE "L" BROOKFIELD ZOO

RUTH HARKNESS FEEDS A BABY SU LIN IN 1936.

The public's excitement when seeing pictures and reading stories about Su Lin set off what people called a panda mania. Zoos across the country were eager to have a live panda on display. From 1936 to 1946, foreigners captured 14 giant pandas and brought them back to their countries. Some of these pandas ended up in the United States. China didn't like that its most honored national treasure was being uprooted from its homeland. So, toward the end of 1946, China stopped allowing anyone to take giant pandas across its borders. Sadly, zoos didn't know enough about how to best care for this exotic animal, and by the early 1950s, all the giant pandas in the United States had died.

Then in 1957, China gave a giant panda named Ping Ping to the Soviet Union as a sign of friendship. Gifts of pandas to other countries, including the United States, followed. Soon China's panda gift giving became known as panda diplomacy. Diplomacy means working out conflicts between countries in a friendly way. This makes sense, since who could get angry at a country that just gave them such an adorable gift?

LING-LING AND HSING-HSING

WHEN PRESIDENT RICHARD NIXON VISITED CHINA in 1972, no panda had set paw in the United States for 20 years. But that changed when the president was given a pair of pandas after his visit. President Nixon's trip was historic because it was the first time that an American president visited mainland China. The visit was a sign of goodwill between the two countries, and China used the gift of giant pandas as a way to strengthen its relationship with the United States.

The two pandas President Nixon received—a female named Ling-Ling and a male named Hsing-Hsing—were given a home at the Smithsonian's National Zoo in Washington, D.C. When they were first put on display, more than 20,000 people visited the famous pair. But that was nothing compared to the following weekend, when 75,000 people stood in a quarter-mile (0.4-km) line to see these adorable bears. During the 23 years of Ling-Ling's life, she gave birth to five cubs, but none of them lived longer than a few days. Hsing-Hsing died at the age of 28 in 1999.

SU LIN AT THE BROOKFIELD ZOO IN ILLINOIS, U.S.A., PHOTOGRAPHED IN 1937.

SU LIN, THE FIRST GIANT PANDA TO COME TO THE UNITED STATES!

LING-LING AND HSING-HSING PLAY AT THE SMITHSONIAN'S NATIONAL ZOO IN WASHINGTON, D.C., IN 1980.

IT'S A PANDA FRUITSICLE CAKE!

PANDA TREATS

GIANT PANDAS IN ZOOS MAINLY EAT BAMBOO, but they also get to eat all sorts of other delicious and nutritious foods, including high-fiber biscuits that supply vitamins and minerals that pandas need. And some pandas in captivity, such as those at the Chengdu Research Base in China, get to eat panda cakes made of corn, soybeans, rice, and oats—yum! The cakes have extra protein, as well as the minerals calcium and phosphorous. Fruits and vegetables, such as apples, yams, and carrots, are also given to captive pandas as treats and are often used as rewards during training.

Rent-a-Panda

By 1982, habitat destruction, along with some hunting, caused the panda population in China to decrease sharply. Suddenly, these black-and-white treasures were endangered and considered to be even more precious. The concern over the dwindling number of pandas spurred China to stop gifting giant pandas to other countries. They started loaning them out instead. In addition to making sure the pandas would eventually be returned to China, the government used the loan program as a way to continue offering the bears as a diplomatic show of goodwill. And that wasn't the only added bonus of the program—these short-term monthly rentals to zoos, including those in the United States, also

HUA MEI, THE FIRST CUB BORN AT THE SAN DIEGO ZOO IN CALIFORNIA, U.S.A., CUDDLES WITH HER MOM, BAI YUN.

became a way for China to make money.

Conservationists fought against these rent-a-panda agreements because the programs contributed to the shrinking number of giant pandas in the wild, and moving these giant pandas to various zoos put them under stress. The other problem was that people still didn't know enough about how to keep pandas healthy in captivity, so many became ill and some died. For these reasons, the United States soon banned the loan programs. But in 1996, the San Diego Zoo struck a different deal with China. For a million dollars a year, China agreed to a 12-year loan of a male and a female giant panda to the San Diego Zoo for research purposes. This began the research and conservation efforts to save China's giant pandas.

TRAINING GIANT PANDAS

WE TRAIN OUR DOGS TO COME WHEN CALLED and to sit and lie down. But can you imagine trying to train a giant panda? You wouldn't think that training giant pandas in zoos or research centers is necessary, but it is. They're not trained to do tricks, though. The people who care for captive pandas need to be able to move them from one place to another, and the giant pandas need to get used to being handled for their medical exams. Giant pandas usually go through two types of training: recall training and target training. The training techniques are similar to those used when training dogs.

Recall training teaches a giant panda to come when called. Trainers use clickers or whistles, or they tap a stick against the enclosure where they want the panda to move. They use food, such as apples or biscuits, to encourage and reward pandas as they master each step in the training process. But don't expect a giant panda to come bounding over when called, like a dog does. Even in zoos and research centers, pandas are the same slow, lumbering bears they are in the wild.

The next step is target training, which teaches animals how to follow a trainer's instructions. Giant pandas are taught to touch their nose to a target, such as a tennis ball on a pole. Again, treats are used as rewards. Once the panda learns to follow instructions, trainers then teach pandas to act in various ways that make caring for them easier. For instance, pandas can learn to hold out their paws for inspection or open their mouth for their teeth to be checked during a veterinary visit.

BAO BAO LEARNS TARGET TRAINING AT THE NATIONAL ZOO IN WASHINGTON, D.C.

A TRAINER TEACHES A PANDA HOW TO STAND UP WHEN ASKED AT THE CHINA CONSERVATION AND RESEARCH CENTER FOR THE GIANT PANDA IN SICHUAN PROVINCE, CHINA.

TWO GIANT PANDAS PLAY AND SNUGGLE.

Panda Matchmakers

It seems nothing a giant panda does is quick and easy. That goes for having cubs, too. Like other bears, the giant panda has only a cub or two every two to three years. This worked well for them for a few million years, before people came into the picture. But now with people bulldozing and chopping away at the panda's habitat, these bears have trouble finding mates. The combination of giving birth to only one or two cubs every couple of years and the scarcity of mates has contributed to the giant panda's decline in population.

To add to this, a female panda is interested in mating just one week a year and is fertile, or

A MALE AND FEMALE PANDA PLAY. KEEPERS HOPE THEY WILL SOMEDAY MATE.

able to get pregnant, during a brief 24- to 72-hour period during that week. For people caring for pandas in captivity, it is difficult to figure out when this fertile period is occurring. Zoos also face the challenge of finding a male and a female panda that want to mate with each other. Pandas in the wild and in captivity can be very choosy when it comes to selecting a mate.

When pandas meet, the male or female panda may not be interested in the other. This is not as much of a problem in the wild because pandas can roam and (hopefully) find other pandas to choose from. But pandas in captivity can't do that. So zoos around the world put their heads together and came up with a possible solution for finding a mate the captive pandas would accept. Zoos decided to mix and match, but not randomly. Scientists figured out which panda pairings would be more likely to produce the healthiest cubs and help make the panda population strong. They started trading giant pandas, hoping to spark love connections. And sometimes, they were successful.

Scientists discovered that the panda's personality traits played a role in breeding success. For example, if they pair a male panda that is more aggressive with a female that is more easygoing, the pair has a better chance of mating and having a cub than if the traits were reversed. And pandas that are attracted to each other are more likely to mate than pandas that feel ho-hum about each other.

Millions of dollars and many hours have been spent in the last 40 years researching and testing ways to help giant pandas mate and reproduce. For a female animal to become pregnant, the male's sperm needs to combine with the female's egg inside her body. This happens naturally through mating. Sometimes people have to get more involved in the process to help a female animal become pregnant. In the case of pandas, veterinarians at zoos and research centers may intervene by injecting a male panda's sperm into a female panda's body in a process that's called artificial insemination. In addition to helping to achieve a pregnancy, this allows scientists to "mate" pandas with traits that will be more likely to produce the strongest and healthiest cub. Although artificial insemination has boosted the giant panda population, it doesn't always result in a pregnancy.

THE CASE OF THE PHANTOM CUB

DEVELOPING CUB

AN ULTRASOUND IMAGE OF A PANDA CUB INSIDE ITS PREGNANT MOTHER

OCCASIONALLY, FEMALE GIANT PANDAS HAVE WHAT'S CALLED A PSEUDOPREGNANCY, or false pregnancy. The pseudo-soon-to-be mom behaves as if she were pregnant. She is less active and moves even more slowly than normal. Because of this, the best way to tell if a female panda is truly pregnant is to do an ultrasound.

An ultrasound produces sound waves that we can't hear. When a sound wave hits an object, it bounces back, much like a bat's use of echolocation. To find out if a giant panda is pregnant, a veterinarian presses an ultrasound device against a giant panda's belly near where a cub might be. The machine sends sound waves into her body and translates the waves that bounce back into a picture. If a panda is pregnant, the ultrasound will show a picture of the developing cub. The only problem is that often the unborn panda cub is too tiny for the ultrasound to pick up.

Scientists are still studying what controls pseudopregnancy in giant pandas, but they do know that they're not the only species that have them. Other mammals, like dogs, can also have pseudopregnancies.

MING MING, SEEN HERE CUDDLING WITH HER MOTHER, WAS BORN SEPTEMBER 9, 1963, AT THE BEIJING ZOO. SHE WAS THE FIRST CUB TO BE BORN IN CAPTIVITY.

MING MING

Any time a female panda in captivity becomes pregnant, it's a huge accomplishment. The news is announced worldwide, and people excitedly wait for the panda cub's birth. Throughout her pregnancy, the mom-to-be is closely watched. She is given extra food, extra attention, and a lot of tests to make sure the pregnancy progresses normally.

Zoo Cubs

If you thought a giant panda's pregnancy was a big deal, just wait until she gives birth. The moment a cub is born in zoos and research centers, it is cared for by a group of keepers, veterinarians, nutritionists, and maybe even some researchers. The first few days are critical to the cub's survival, and in the past,

many cubs born in captivity died soon after birth. Today, zoos and research centers have become better at helping these babies survive to be the black-and-white pudgy roly-polies that have stolen our hearts.

The breeding programs in China produce most of the giant panda cubs that are born in captivity. The China Conservation and Research Center for the Giant Panda (CCRCGP) in central China's Sichuan Province has had the most success with breeding pandas. A record-breaking 44 panda cubs were born there in 2017. Talk about cuteness overload!

One reason the captive panda breeding program has become so successful is because the scientists at the Chengdu Zoo in China have made a breakthrough in caring for twins. Whether in the wild or in zoos, about half of the giant pandas that have cubs give birth to twins. Newborn giant panda cubs require a lot of attention. Remember, they're born tiny and underdeveloped, so they need more care than the average newborn bear. Mother pandas usually don't have enough milk to feed more than one cub. A giant panda that gives birth to twins in the wild can't give them both the care they need, so usually only one of the twins survives. But in captivity, people can lend a hand. Caretakers help the mother by swapping out one of the panda twins so each cub gets a turn getting Mom's milk and care. This breakthrough method seems simple, but the caretakers have to be sneaky to make this work and not upset the mom.

When twins are born, a caretaker waits until the mother panda places one of the cubs on the floor to care for the other cub. Then the caretaker quickly but gently takes the cub that's on the floor before the mother notices.

After being taken from its mother, the twin is placed in an incubator, a cozy crib that keeps the newborn warm and safe. This is when veterinarians have the chance to weigh the cub, give it a checkup, and bottle feed it formula to make sure it's getting all the nutrients it needs. The twins continue to be swapped until they are able to eat solid food on their own, at about six or seven months.

The team of people caring for the twins keep a close eye on them as they grow, periodically recording their weight, height, and how much food they eat. All this care has boosted the survival rate of giant panda cubs to 98 percent.

A NEWBORN PANDA DRINKS FROM A BOTTLE.

THE NAME GAME

ACCORDING TO CHINESE TRADITION, giant panda cubs need to be 100 days old before they're given a name. It's believed that if a cub lives to a hundred days, the newborn is likely to survive. Zoos across the United States follow this tradition and frequently hold naming contests for their panda cubs during the 100-day wait. But the name needs to be approved by Chinese authorities before it becomes official.

NEWBORN PANDA AND MOM, SHUQIN, AT THE CHINA CONSERVATION AND RESEARCH CENTER FOR THE GIANT PANDA IN SICHUAN PROVINCE, CHINA

THIS CUB WON'T BE NAMED FOR 100 DAYS.

Home Again

Some good things don't last forever, and that's true of the giant pandas sent to zoos outside of China. Since every giant panda in zoos around the world is on loan from China, the time will come when it will need to return to its homeland. When that is depends on the loan agreement. China can extend the loan, as it did with Bai Yun at the San Diego Zoo. This female panda came to the United States as a five-year-old in 1996 on a 12-year loan, and as of 2018 she is still in the country. Bai Yun is famous for being the mother of six of the giant panda cubs born in the United States that have survived past infancy.

As part of China's panda loan agreement, panda cubs born outside of the country head back to China to join a breeding program, usually by the time they're four years old. Even though Bai Yun has stayed in the United States, all her cubs have been transported back to China. The panda youngsters fly in style on small jets equipped with cool air, a nice cozy enclosure, and a lot of water and food, including bamboo, of course. They also get treats of apples, pears, and vegetables such as cooked sweet potatoes and carrots. The young pandas are constantly watched for distress and any slight change in their behavior. Every comfort is offered to these VIPs—very important pandas.

Once the giant pandas arrive in China, they are quarantined for a month before being taken to a research center or breeding facility. During that month, they are kept in living areas separate from other pandas to make sure they're not sick. The quarantine also reduces

BAI YUN CRUNCHES ON A CARROT AT THE SAN DIEGO ZOO IN CALIFORNIA, U.S.A.

THE PANDA EXPRESS HAS ARRIVED! A FEDEX PLANE LANDS IN EDINBURGH, SCOTLAND, U.K., WITH PANDAS TIAN TIAN AND YANG GUANG ABOARD.

the likelihood of disease spreading to the other pandas. These youngsters are not introduced into the wild because they don't have the skills they need to survive. Instead, they remain part of the breeding population in China and serve as ambassadors to the visitors who come from all over the world. But they still have some hurdles to overcome when adjusting to life in China.

One important hurdle is that giant pandas need to learn Chinese. You wouldn't think this would be a big deal since they're pandas, but all the training these pandas received was in the host country's native language. In the United States, for example, pandas are trained in English. When someone says "Come" to a panda, it comes toddling over. But when that command is given in Chinese, the pandas don't understand.

Food can be a problem, too. Pandas in captivity are given a variety of foods. We already know that bamboo is the giant panda's main food—whether in China or in the zoos in other countries. But the kind of bamboo fed to pandas often differs from one country to the next. And just as you're used to your American diet and may have difficulty adapting to Chinese food, the same goes for giant pandas that have to adapt to a different diet. Besides getting used to a different variety of bamboo, giant pandas that enjoyed eating biscuits while in the United States need to learn to like the panda cake they get served in China. Thankfully, the people who work with the pandas in China are patient and understanding. They do everything they can to help pandas get used to their new life.

TAI SHAN AT THE NATIONAL ZOO IN WASHINGTON, D.C., A FEW DAYS BEFORE HE IS FLOWN TO CHINA. IN THE BACKGROUND IS THE SPECIAL SHIPPING CRATE THAT WILL CARRY HIM SAFELY ON HIS TRIP HOME.

BECOME A PANDA RESEARCHER

MOST CAREERS THAT HELP PANDAS require at least a four-year college degree in a science field such as biology, ecology, or zoology. **BIOLOGY** is the study of living organisms and how they grow. **ECOLOGY** is the study of how living organisms interact with their environment. And **ZOOLOGY** is the study of animals. If you want to work on a breeding program, you may need to study **GENETICS** or even **VETERINARY MEDICINE**. Earning a degree in **LAND MANAGEMENT** could also get you working with giant pandas. People trained in land management, like our explorer Marc Brody, help researchers figure out how to restore and manage habitat for animals, including pandas.

You don't need to wait until college to start preparing for a career with pandas. You can begin right now by getting involved in after-school and summer programs that focus on these science topics. Take a lot of science courses to prepare for college, and volunteer with a local environmental club, wildlife rehabilitation center, zoo, or animal shelter. This will help you decide if working outside with animals is something that you would like to do.

STUDY LAND MANAGEMENT TO HELP RESTORE HABITATS—AND BE AN EXPLORER LIKE MARC BRODY.

BE A BIOLOGIST—STUDY LIVING ORGANISMS.

BE A ZOOLOGIST—STUDY ANIMALS.

STUDY VETERINARY MEDICINE AND FOCUS ON REPRODUCTION, LIKE DR. DAVID KERSEY, WHO HELPED THESE PANDAS TO BE BORN AT ZOO ATLANTA IN 2013.

BE AN ECOLOGIST—STUDY HOW ORGANISMS INTERACT WITH THE ENVIRONMENT.

BE A GENETICIST—STUDY GENES AND HEREDITY.

AFTER TWO YEARS OF REINTRODUCTION TRAINING, XUE XUE IS RELEASED INTO THE WILD AT LIZIPING NATURE RESERVE IN SHIMIAN, SICHUAN PROVINCE, CHINA.

A Walk Back to the Wild Side

In July of 2003, hoping to use all they had learned about caring for pandas in captivity, scientists were ready to take the next step toward saving the giant panda. It was time to start introducing captive-born pandas to their wild and natural habitat. But you can't just take animals that have been raised in captivity and send them off into the forest. They wouldn't know what to do. Giant pandas raised in captivity don't have to forage, or search, for their food or water. They just sit back and grab a bamboo culm from the pile on the ground. There is never any shortage of food. In captivity, pandas are kept in their own enclosures, free from predators, so they don't have to learn how to defend themselves. All their needs are met. It became clear to scientists that captive giant pandas would have to learn how to live in the wild.

To jump-start this effort, scientists at CCRCGP gathered a team of experts to study how captive pandas adjust to life in the wild. These experts wanted to learn what it would take to train pandas to successfully live in their natural habitat.

A two-year-old male panda named Xiang Xiang was chosen to go through a three-year training program. Xiang Xiang was taught how to forage for his own food and find water. He was released into the wild in April 2006. Sadly, less than a year later, in February 2007, Xiang Xiang was found dead. He had some wounds and broken bones, so researchers thought he may have fought with other male pandas or fallen from a tree. Scientists needed to come up with a better program to help these animals live successfully in the wild.

The scientists at CCRCGP spent the next several years doing further studies to improve their reintroduction program. They chose more appropriate areas to reintroduce the pandas, and they decided to limit or eliminate any human

THE VIEW FROM ABOVE THE SHENSHUPING GIANT PANDA PROTECTION BASE OF WOLONG NATURE RESERVE IN SICHUAN PROVINCE, CHINA

RESEARCHERS DRESSED AS PANDAS GENTLY PLACE THE CUB TAO TAO INTO A BASKET TO TAKE HIM FOR A WALK IN THE WOLONG NATURE RESERVE IN SICHUAN PROVINCE, CHINA.

contact with the giant pandas that were chosen to be released into the wild. Scientists wanted to be sure that the pandas would learn to gather food, water, and be able to take care of any of their other needs on their own. They wanted the pandas to fear people as they would in the wild. Now any person interacting with a giant panda had to wear a panda suit, including a panda mask. The people also had to be covered in panda pee and poop to hide human odor.

In 2010, four pregnant giant pandas were moved to a remote area of the Wolong Nature Reserve. The pandas were kept in a large outdoor enclosure in natural panda habitat. Although the pandas would feel as though they were living a wild life, scientists could still keep a close watch on them using cameras placed around the enclosure. The plan worked. On August 3, 2010, a male cub,

CAO CAO MOVES INTO A LARGER ENCLOSURE AT THE WOLONG NATURE RESERVE.

eventually named Tao Tao, was born. And he was born without any help from people. His mother, Cao Cao, was a captive panda that had been born in the wild. So scientists decided that since Cao Cao had experience living in the wild, this mama-cub pair would be the best candidates for reintroduction into the wild.

Cao Cao was left alone with Tao Tao to raise him on her own. But scientists continued to watch them carefully. When Tao Tao was one month old, he and Cao Cao were moved to a larger enclosure with more than a hundred cameras set up for scientists to keep tabs on the pair. Here, mother and cub had to work a bit harder to find food and water, and the risks to Tao Tao were a bit higher, with more dangers, such as the possibility of encountering other animals. But this was a necessary step in the reintroduction process. Every day, Cao Cao

TAO TAO TAKES A STROLL!

TAO TAO SLOWLY MAKES HIS WAY TOWARD A BAMBOO FOREST IN THE REINTRODUCTION AREA.

was teaching Tao Tao how to live in the wild.

In May of 2012, when Tao Tao was almost two years old, mother and son were moved to the final stage of the reintroduction program. They were taken to an even larger enclosure that was higher up the mountain. This time, sound recordings of other wild animals were played as a way to get Tao Tao to recognize and avoid his natural enemies, such as leopards.

One and a half is the minimum age young giant pandas leave their mother. In October 2012, shortly after his second birthday, Tao Tao was fitted with a GPS collar so he could be tracked and further studied after his release into the wild. October 11, 2012, was the historic day that Tao Tao was taken to the Xiaoxiangling Mountains and released at the Liziping Nature Reserve at Shimian, Ya'an, in Sichuan Province. In December of 2017, five years after he first set

A RESEARCHER CARRIES TAO TAO TO A NEW LOCATION IN THE REINTRODUCTION AREA.

off into the mountains, Tao Tao was recaptured and thoroughly examined. Veterinarians found him to be in perfect health and at a good weight. They replaced the tracking chip on his collar and let him trudge back into the wild. Tao Tao's release was a success, and scientists were thrilled.

After Tao Tao's initial release, plans for reintroducing giant pandas to the wild continued. Over the following five years, eight more pandas were trained and released into the wild. Seven of them are still alive. And with the establishment of the huge panda national park that will link 67 fragmented reserves into one big reserve, reintroductions of pandas to the wild will most likely be even more successful. Pandas will be able to roam farther and breed with other pandas in the park, which will strengthen the health of the species.

SCIENTISTS IN CHINA ARE BUSY taking care of giant pandas and working to increase their numbers. Take a closer look at five of these reserves and research centers.

THE WOLONG NATURE RESERVE IS CHINA'S FIRST AND MOST FAMOUS giant panda reserve. It was established in 1963. Some of the buildings had to be rebuilt after a huge earthquake in 2008 shook Sichuan Province. The earthquake was so massive that its impact pushed the ground about 23 feet (7 m) high in some places.

WOLONG NATURE RESERVE

GENGDA GIANT PANDA CENTER

BIFENGXIA GIANT PANDA BASE (BFX)

THE GENGDA GIANT PANDA CENTER WAS BUILT ON THE WOLONG NATURE RESERVE after much of the reserve was destroyed in the 2008 earthquake. It has a research laboratory and panda hospital and 59 indoor-outdoor enclosures, and nearby are three 10- to 30-acre (4- to 12-ha) panda reintroduction enclosures. Besides being used for research, captive breeding, and reintroducing pandas to the wild, Gengda is open to the public. People can observe pandas there and learn more about them.

CHENGDU RESEARCH BASE OF GIANT PANDA BREEDING

THE 247-ACRE (100-HA) CHENGDU RESEARCH BASE OF GIANT PANDA BREEDING is known for protecting and breeding wild animal species that are unique to China, including giant pandas. As of early 2017, the base was caring for and breeding 176 giant pandas, the largest group of artificially bred pandas in the world.

THE BIFENGXIA GIANT PANDA BASE (BFX) was built during 2002–2003 and covers 988 acres (400 ha). It took in pandas that had been evacuated from the Hetaoping Wolong Panda Center because of the 2008 earthquake. Today, BFX has probably the cutest attraction: a panda kindergarten. People can visit and watch panda cubs get weighed, fed, and cared for in other ways.

DUJIANGYAN PANDA BASE

THE DUJIANGYAN PANDA BASE IS A BUSY PLACE. Besides housing a panda hospital and 40 enclosures, it also offers an educational center. The hospital cares for injured giant pandas found in the wild and for older giant pandas. This is where pandas traveling in and out of China stay to be quarantined, to make sure they're not sick or carrying any diseases. The Dujiangyan Panda Base offers a volunteer program in which people can help giant panda caretakers.

AERIAL VIEW OF THE SHAANXI RARE WILDLIFE RESCUE AND BREEDING RESEARCH CENTRE IN SHAANXI PROVINCE, CHINA

THANKS TO RESEARCHERS AND CONSERVATIONISTS, PANDAS ARE NO LONGER ON THE RED LIST OF THREATENED SPECIES—BUT THEY STILL NEED OUR HELP!

KAI KAI NIBBLING ON BAMBOO AT THE SINGAPORE ZOO, SINGAPORE

To the Rescue

Though captive panda breeding and reintroduction programs are promising, these animals are not out of danger. Shrinking habitat is still a major concern, especially when factoring in the potential effects of climate change. And even though pandas have been downlisted on the Red List of Threatened Species to "vulnerable," some people believe wild pandas are still in danger of becoming extinct. They point to the inconsistent ways that giant pandas in the wild have been counted. They say some survey methods, such as getting DNA from feces, are unreliable, and the politics of government and conservation groups often influence the results, leading to inaccurate counts. These critics claim that no one really knows how many of the shy, hard-to-find bears are hiding in China's mountain forests. Some fear that it may have been too soon to take them off the endangered species list. Because of this uncertainty, they want people to continue working hard to save giant pandas and their habitat.

China is doing more to protect the giant panda by working to establish the new Giant Panda National Park and by supporting the Wolong Nature Reserve and its sister organization, the CCRCGP, which has a total of four panda bases now. These bases serve giant pandas in various ways, including housing laboratories for scientific research, supporting captive breeding programs, reintroducing pandas to the wild, and educating the public.

China isn't alone in its drive to save the giant panda. Worldwide, scientists, conservationists, zoos, governments, and regular people are working hard to help this iconic animal move farther away from the brink of extinction. With the help of new research and increased efforts, people are approaching the problem in different ways. While some scientists are working on making panda breeding programs even more successful, conservationists are turning their attention to restoring the panda's habitat back to the large strips of forested land filled with the wide variety of plants and animals it once had.

The giant panda is China's national treasure and ambassador to the rest of the world. This black-and-white bear has shown us how to balance power and peacefulness, and has captured our hearts like few other animals ever have. Efforts to save the panda and its habitat continue to have far-reaching effects on countless plants and animals that are, like the panda, struggling to survive in a warming world with shrinking natural habitats and resources. Anything we do to help restore and conserve natural lands will help giant pandas and other wildlife live well into the future.

A PANDA CLIMBS UP HIGH TO ENJOY THE VIEW.

A GIANT PANDA CUB IS WEIGHED AT THE BIFENGXIA GIANT PANDA BASE IN SICHUAN PROVINCE, CHINA.

PANDA HABITAT PAST AND PRESENT

MOST OF THE WORLD'S WILD PANDAS live in 67 nature reserves in China's old-growth forests. The rest of the wild pandas roam in unprotected areas nearby. China has been creating reserves to restore and protect disappearing panda habitat, increasing the bears' geographic range by almost 12 percent since 2003. These are the same protected areas where captive-bred pandas are being reintroduced into the wild.

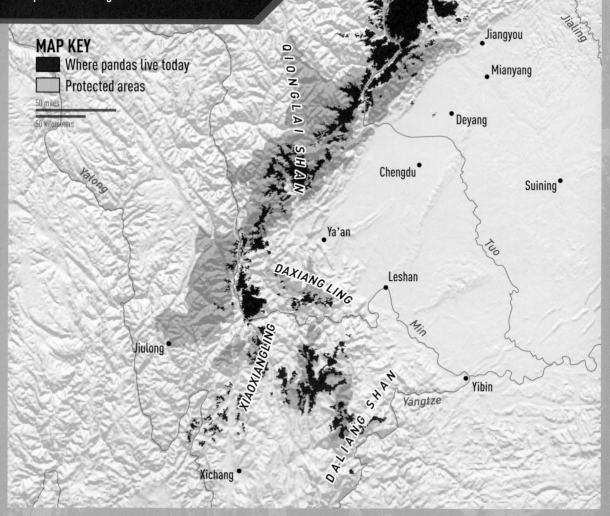

MAP KEY
- Where pandas live today
- Protected areas

50 miles
50 kilometers

MIN SHAN

Guangyuan

Jiangyou

Mianyang

Jialing

QIONGLAI SHAN

Deyang

Chengdu

Suining

Yalong

Ya'an

Tuo

DAXIANG LING

Leshan

Min

Jiulong

XIAOXIANGLING

DALIANG SHAN

Yibin

Yangtze

Xichang

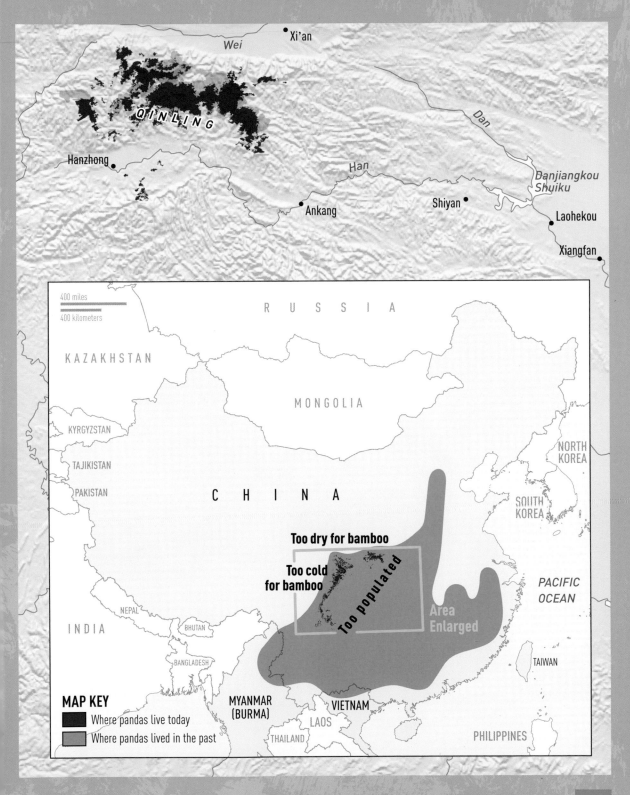

Wei

Xi'an

QINLING

Dan

Hanzhong

Han

Danjiangkou
Shuiku

Ankang

Shiyan

Laohekou

Xiangfan

400 miles

400 kilometers

RUSSIA

KAZAKHSTAN

MONGOLIA

KYRGYZSTAN

TAJIKISTAN

PAKISTAN

C H I N A

NORTH
KOREA

SOUTH
KOREA

Too dry for bamboo

Too cold
for bamboo

Too populated

Area
Enlarged

PACIFIC
OCEAN

NEPAL

BHUTAN

INDIA

BANGLADESH

TAIWAN

MYANMAR
(BURMA)

VIETNAM

LAOS

PHILIPPINES

THAILAND

MAP KEY

Where pandas live today

Where pandas lived in the past

PANDA-MAZING!

MAKE YOUR OWN PANDA TREATS

Use your next celebration as a way to honor giant pandas by making mini-panda treats! Grab an adult and head to the kitchen to make these Mini–Giant Panda Cupcakes.

What you need:

1 12-OZ BAG CHOCOLATE CHIPS

48 MINI-CUPCAKE BAKING CUPS (PAPER OR REUSABLE)

Cake Mix
Super Moist
Family Size
All Natural

1 BOX VANILLA CUPCAKE MIX

MINI-CUPCAKE OR MINI-MUFFIN PAN

BLACK OR CHOCOLATE SPRINKLES

WHITE FROSTING

SHREDDED COCONUT

ASK A GROWN-UP TO HELP YOU BAKE YOUR PANDA CUPCAKES!

What to do:

1. Ask a grown-up to help you follow the instructions on the box to make your cupcakes.

2. Once your cupcakes have cooled, top them with white frosting. This is going to be your panda face.

3. Pour the shredded coconut into a bowl.

4. Dip your cupcake, frosting side down, into the coconut. You can use your clean hands to gently press the coconut into the frosting. You want the coconut to give your panda a furry look.

5. Take two chocolate chips and press them point side down and edge first into the frosting for the ears. The smooth underside of the chocolate chips should be facing toward you.

6. Take two more chocolate chips and press them point side down into the frosting where the panda's eyes should be.

7. Take another chocolate chip and press it sideways into the frosting where the nose should be. Make sure the tip of the chip is pointing down toward the panda's mouth.

FROST YOUR CUPCAKE WITH WHITE FROSTING BEFORE YOU DIP IT IN THE SHREDDED COCONUT.

8. Use the sprinkles to make a smile under the nose. Experiment with placing the sprinkles at other angles to create different panda expressions.

9. Step back and admire your artistry, then enjoy your special treat!

ADD A DOT OF WHITE FROSTING TO CHOCOLATE CHIP EYES AND PLACE A MINI CHOCOLATE CHIP ON TOP FOR A MORE EXPRESSIVE FACE.

GLOSSARY

BAMBOO SHOOT: New growth of bamboo from the bamboo's rhizome, also a favorite food of giant pandas

BIODIVERSITY: A wide variety of plants and animals in a habitat or ecosystem

CANOPY: The second tallest layer of growth in a forest, usually made of leafy deciduous trees that block the sun and protect the plants below from the wind

CCRCGP: Abbreviation for the China Conservation and Research Center for the Giant Panda

CLIMATE CHANGE: A change in weather patterns over a long period of time

CONIFER: Trees that have needles and cones. Most conifers are evergreen trees.

CRITICALLY ENDANGERED: IUCN category indicating a species that is at extremely high risk of becoming extinct in the wild

CULM: The woody stem of a bamboo plant that is hollow and flexible

EMERGENT LAYER: The tallest layer of plants in a forest

ENDANGERED: IUCN category indicating a species that is at high risk of becoming extinct in the wild

EROSION: The process of wind, water, or glaciers wearing away and moving rocks, minerals, soil, and small plants from one place to another

EXTINCT: IUCN category indicating the last living individual of the species has died; the species no longer exists.

EXTINCT IN THE WILD: IUCN category indicating individuals of a species can no longer be found living in the wild but live in captivity or in an area outside their normal range

DECIDUOUS: Trees that lose their leaves in the fall

DNA: An abbreviation for deoxyribonucleic acid. It partly controls the individual characteristics of all living beings.

INTERNODE: A section of the bamboo culm. Internodes are hollow and separated by solid rings called nodes.

IUCN: Abbreviation for the International Union for Conservation of Nature

LEAST CONCERN: IUCN category indicating that a species does not qualify for any of the other categories

MAMMAL: A classification of animal with the following characteristics: warm-blooded, vertebrate, has hair or fur, produces milk for its babies, and typically gives birth to live young

NATURE RESERVE: A protected area of land with the purpose of supporting the wildlife, plants, and geological features within; also referred to as a nature preserve

NEAR THREATENED: IUCN category indicating a species that doesn't qualify as critically endangered, endangered, or vulnerable but is soon likely to qualify

NODE: A solid ring on a bamboo culm that separates the hollow internodes and from which bamboo branches grow

OMNIVORE: An animal that eats everything, including other animals and plants

PERENNIALS: Plants that live through two or more growing seasons

PIGEON-TOED: A person's or animal's feet that turn toward each other

PSEUDO: False or looking like something else

RHIZOME: A plant stem that grows underground, producing roots that grow into the ground and shoots that grow above ground

SCAT: Animal poop

SHOOTING SEASON: The time in spring when bamboo shoots start to grow

TAXIDERMY: Using an animal skin to create a lifelike representation of the animal in its natural form

UMAMI: The distinct savory flavor used to describe the taste of food high in protein such as meat

UNDERSTORY: The layer of plants and trees that is above the forest floor and below the canopy. Bamboo is the understory in panda habitat.

VERTEBRATE: An animal with a spine

VULNERABLE: IUCN category indicating a species that is at risk of extinction due to a significant reduction of its population and habitat fragmentation

FOR MORE GIANT PANDAS:

Jazynka, Kitson. *Mission Panda Rescue: All About Pandas and How to Save Them*. National Geographic Kids, 2016.

NATIONAL GEOGRAPHIC KIDS:
GIANT PANDA FACTS AND PICTURES WEBSITE
natgeokids.com/animals/giant-panda

PANDA MOUNTAIN WEBSITE
pandamountain.org

WORLD WILDLIFE FUND (WWF) PANDA WEBSITE
worldwildlife.org/species/giant-panda

INDEX

Boldface indicates photos or illustrations.

IMAGE CREDITS

To the next generation of conservationists who will help restore habitat to save endangered species around the world. —MB

For young conservationists and all those who work hard to protect nature and help animals and plants thrive. —RS

Since 1888, the National Geographic Society has funded more than 12,000 research, exploration, and preservation projects around the world. The Society receives funds from National Geographic Partners, LLC, funded in part by your purchase. A portion of the proceeds from this book supports this vital work. To learn more, visit natgeo.com/info.

For more information, visit nationalgeographic.com, call 1-800-647-5463, or write to the following address:

National Geographic Partners
1145 17th Street N.W.
Washington, D.C. 20036-4688 U.S.A.

Visit us online at nationalgeographic.com/books

For librarians and teachers: ngchildrensbooks.org

More for kids from National Geographic: natgeokids.com

National Geographic Kids magazine inspires children to explore their world with fun yet educational articles on animals, science, nature, and more. Using fresh storytelling and amazing photography, *Nat Geo Kids* shows kids ages 6 to 14 the fascinating truth about the world—and why they should care.
kids.nationalgeographic.com/subscribe

For information about special discounts for bulk purchases, please contact National Geographic Books Special Sales: specialsales@natgeo.com

For rights or permissions inquiries, please contact National Geographic Books Subsidiary Rights: bookrights@natgeo.com

Designed by Girl Friday Productions

National Geographic supports K–12 educators with ELA Common Core Resources. Visit natgeoed.org/commoncore for more information.

Library of Congress Cataloging-in-Publication Data
Names: National Geographic Society (U.S.)
Title: Absolute expert : pandas / by National Geographic Kids.
Description: Pandas | Series: Absolute expert | Includes index. |
   Audience: Age 8-12. | Audience: Grade 4 to 6.
Identifiers: LCCN 2018057541| ISBN 9781426334313 (paperback) |
   ISBN 9781426334320 (hardcover)
Subjects: LCSH: Giant panda--Juvenile literature.
Classification: LCC QL737.C27 A27 2019 | DDC 599.789--dc23
LC record available at https://lccn.loc.gov/2018057541

Acknowledgments

Thanks to Panda Mountain's volunteers who have supported Wolong Nature Reserve, to the Thoresen Foundation for their financial support, and a special thanks to Mr. Zhang Hemin ("Papa Panda") for making our panda conservation work in Wolong possible. —MB

Many thanks to the talented people at Girl Friday Productions and National Geographic, with special thanks to Kristin Mehus-Roe, Karen Upson, Leah Jenness, Priyanka Lamichhane, and Angela Modany. —RS

The publisher would like to thank Dr. David Kersey for contributing his expertise to this book. From Girl Friday Productions, the publisher would like to thank: Karen Upson, project editor; Micah Schmidt, photo research; and Rachel Marek, designer. And from National Geographic Partners: Angela Modany, associate editor; Amanda Larsen, design director; Sarah J. Mock, senior photo editor; Mike McNey, map production; Sean Philpotts, production director; Anne LeongSon and Gus Tello, design production assistants; Sally Abbey, managing editor; and Molly Reid, production editor.

Printed in Hong Kong
19/PPHK/1

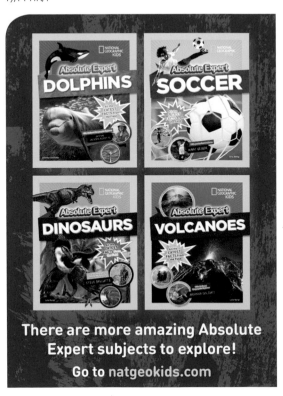